From the pages of Buzz Ride

Late Thursday had become Friday. At one-thirty in the morning, I got buzzed. I stared at the phone. *Do I really want to take this, or should I head home?* Oh, what the hell. It would be an easy local shot and I'd be home by two. A couple minutes later I was pulling up to a bar behind Wrigley Field. Two young white guys opened the back door, threw a girl in her early twenties into my back seat, and ran away.

Note to self: It is never good when someone throws a fare into the car and runs away. She was a chunky little cherub. She lifted herself off the floor of the car and chirped happily, "Hello. Who are you?"

I had gambled and I had lost. This already didn't appear to be that last easy money trip I had expected. "Where do you wish to be taken?"

"I don't know my address," she replied and laughed, falling back into the car's rear seat.

"Alright," I said, taking a deep breath. "Can I see your driver's license, so we can read your address and get you home?"

"I only have my debit card," she laughed again in reply. She told me to just drive up and down streets and she would recognize her house. I drove up Addison and my passenger went from a giggly little drunk to a little terror—and a character in one of my future worst nightmares—shouting, "This isn't it!" I turned down Sheffield, and she yelled, "No, you idiot, this isn't it either!" I cautioned myself to keep everything calm because this was getting very uncomfortable. She sat up, and the cherub returned. Leaning forward and rubbing my right shoulder, she said, "You remind me of my daddy."

This isn't good, Pat thought and he kindly told her not to touch him.

The mean girl reappeared. "Are you getting weird with me?"

There I was driving around at two a.m. with some girl young enough to be my daughter and drunk enough to not know where she lived. I pleaded with her to focus and remember her address. She blurted out, "Something to do with a lot of fucking trees." Great. Now I was playing charades with a smashed member of the purple-dinosaur generation in the wee hours.

As if it weren't already bad enough, she was starting to fall asleep, and I wasn't any closer to knowing where this bundle of irresponsibility lived. She nodded off, and I was driving aimlessly through the early morning with one clue. "Something to do with a lot of fucking trees," Patrick muttered.

BUZZ RIDE

DRIVEN TO DISRUPTION

MEMOIRS OF AN UBER DRIVER

By P.M. White

Lake Claremont Press: A Chicago Joint

LAKE CLAREMONT PRESS
— a Chicago Joint —

Chicago ▪ Milwaukee

Buzz Ride: Driven to Disruption: Memoirs of an Uber Driver
P.M. White

LAKE CLAREMONT PRESS
—— a Chicago Joint ——

Lake Claremont Press: A Chicago Joint, an imprint of Everything Goes Media, LLC
www.lakeclaremont.com
www.everythinggoesmedia.com

Published August 2017

Publisher's Cataloging-In-Publication Data
(Prepared by The Donohue Group, Inc.)

Names: White, P. M., 1957-
Title: Buzz ride : driven to disruption : memoirs of an Uber driver / by P.M. White.
Description: Chicago ; Milwaukee : Lake Claremont Press, a Chicago joint, [2017] | Previously published: Indianapolis, IN : Dog Ear Publishing, [2015]. | Includes bibliographical references.
Identifiers: LCCN 2017934784 | ISBN 978-1-893121-66-9 (print) | ISBN 978-1-893121-59-1 (ebook)
Subjects: LCSH: White, P. M., 1957- | Ridesharing--Illinois--Chicago. | Ridesharing--Anecdotes. | Uber (Firm) | Automobile drivers--Illinois--Chicago. | Businesspeople--Illinois--Chicago. | Chicago (Ill.)--Social conditions--21st century.
Classification: LCC HE5620.R53 W55 2017 (print) | LCC HE5620.R53 (ebook) | DDC 388.4/1321--dc23

21 20 19 18 17   10 9 8 7 6 5 4 3 2 1

Book design by Mike Wykowski. Front cover design by P-Squared Creative Consulting (nick@p-squaredcreativeconsulting.com).

Editing by Rose Kaiser, Rebecca Straple, and Sharon Woodhouse.

*To all who have sacrificed so much to give all Americans
the freedoms to try, to fail, and to succeed.*

Thank you for your service.

PREFACE

I spent over thirty years toiling in the financial world and investment industry, always trying to stay current with ever-changing business trends, so it's no surprise that I was drawn to the new disruptive technologies affecting commerce. All the discussion in the business news about the new rideshare concept intrigued me, and I also found out that this mode of transportation was the chauffeur of choice for young adults in urban areas. Ultimately, my curiosity about how young adults in their twenties and thirties navigate through life with the power of the smart phone led me on an interesting journey.

In the spring of 2014 I realized it had been some time since I had last been published in a business journal. Plus, the trust with which young adults relied on handheld devices to transact business and do their banking now gave me an interesting topic for a research paper. How many ecommerce applications does the average Millennial use? What is the average dollar amount of their transactions? Do they pay all their bills online? Do they ever get nervous accessing their bank accounts in cyberspace? These were questions that I wanted answered.

Little did I know that the original quest for knowledge would be scrapped for a journal recalling the shocking events and provocative conversations that would take place in the backseat of my car.

I needed to find a way to be able to do hands-on research and mine for data. I quickly realized that the confines of an automobile gave me the rolling research laboratory I needed. To my amazement and the chagrin of the regulated taxi industry, I learned that anyone with a fairly late model four-door car, driver's license, clean background check, and car insurance can go into business as a for-hire rideshare driver. In addition to the previously mentioned requirements, the driver undergoes a ten-minute online tutorial and takes quizzes that serve as the prospective driver's training. No chauffer's license needed—just a decent whip (a term the youngsters use for car), a full tank of gas, and a one-application smart phone supplied by the rideshare company.

The curiosity and need for data haunted me. I live in Chicago, Illinois, which is diverse in neighborhoods and at present leads the nation in gun violence. For weeks, I vacillated between the risks and merits of satisfying my curiosity. I considered what my friends and family would think and of my professional status in the business world. I had been the president of two companies and managed money for some of Hollywood's top celebrities. I had an MBA from a prestigious institution. I had been the member of a well-respected city club for over thirty years, and most importantly, I'm a father in my fifties. What the hell was I thinking? Still, my curiosity and the need for quantifiable data was insatiable.

I began working at a very young age and have had many different jobs. I've waited tables, drilled bowling balls, strung tennis rackets, cleaned dog runs, pumped gas, painted houses, detailed cars, loaded produce onto trucks, and was even a night orderly in an alcoholic rehabilitation center, to name a few. I was raised with the philosophy that there is no shame in honest work. During high school and college, I attacked having a job with reckless abandonment—so reckless that I pumped gas during the night at a secluded gas station surrounded by a forest preserve. I found out a few years later that the customer who would come in on the weekends and irritate me and make me feel uncomfortable was none other than John Wayne Gacy. In retrospect, I realize someone was looking out for me, and thankfully I wasn't the sick clown's type. Early in my professional life, I realized that all those jobs, bosses, and customers helped give me a broad foundation for the rest of my business career. And that that has been beneficial.

One of the most difficult aspects of my experience with rideshare were its mental challenges and making the transition from being an executive to being someone's driver. It was awkward at first, but those challenges transmuted into a rebirth of my beliefs in some fundamental business principles—tenets formed by the raw, in-the-trenches experiences of an ambitious and energetic young man of many years ago. The inner competitive being that fought fierce business rivals in boardrooms was emerging in my effort to be the most efficient, highly-rated, and profitable Uber driver on the road. Situations and experiences that had been dormant in my memory began to resurface, as did a youthful curiosity about life. In an era when motivational consulting firms give workshops on trust and inner growth, I now see the merit of a retrospective, back-to-the-fundamentals learning experience for those who may be out of touch with what made them who they are. The ability to set pride and ego aside and to become a receptacle for new ideas, methods, and experiences wakens the thirst to learn that may have been buried by life's monotonous odyssey. This exercise was humbling and exhilarating, while first and foremost at times, terrifying.

Even as a lifelong, well-traveled Chicagoan, every night I would see something fascinating and new, including spectacular homes and neighborhoods buried down streets that I didn't normally travel. I became acquainted with the hot nightspots and the quaint, local corner taverns that seem to be in every neighborhood. I explored Wicker Park, Humboldt Park, Englewood, the Viagra Triangle, Division Street, the Gold Coast, and all points in between. Many of these neighborhoods are Chicago beauties...and have been invaded by recent college graduates from small towns all over the Midwest, in the big city on their own away from Mom and Dad and ripping it hard on the streets.

My tale conveys some of the mating habits of these techno-brats as they do what my generation did, only in a digital age. The events this book shares will take you on a nocturnal trip to a young adult fantasy amusement park virtually augmented in the real world, with all the fears and concerns that have plagued urban America for decades. Watching all this unfold from the driver's seat made me realize that people can be raw and deplorable, as well as the fact that my generation may not even be relevant. I will share with you the drunken, stoned debauchery that took place in my Mercedes, encompassing more than 600 fares over more than three months in the spring and summer of 2014. You might get tired of hearing, "Hey, dude (which became my new name). I've never been picked up in a Benz before. Any extra charge?" The answer would be no, and their response? "Cool, dude."

Admittedly, I intentionally drove in the neighborhoods and at the peak times in which the young adults of the city played. I went looking for partying and uninhibited behavior, and I found it. I've had many great sales mentors in my life who have taught me advanced profiling techniques that, at times, gave me the ability to delve a bit deeper into a topic than most rideshare drivers. Barriers got broken down and verbal inhibitions were shed, making this trek a true educational experience for this older, worldly man. My weekend nights for three months made reality television look tame.

Three things inspired the title of the book. The first is the sound that one of the smart phone applications makes when there is a fare waiting. The second is the condition of the majority of my passengers. They were either over-served at the local club or buzzed on some other substance. Third was the pleasant annoyance of my buzzing Taser—hence *Buzz Ride*.

BUZZ
RIDE

TRANSFORMATION

The City of Big Shoulders was slowly defrosting from one of the worst winter seasons in more than twenty years. A new term had entered every Chicagoan's vocabulary: polar vortex. The city was a long way from recovering from the relentless snowplowing and the asphalt-decaying salt that left the roads in many neighborhoods looking like they had been bombed, posing a serious risk to the safety and welfare of all who traveled on them. But none of that mattered much because it was finally spring in Chicago—though spring had not quite rushed to the rescue. The month of May was cold and even saw some late snow flurries. While the Chicago Cubs were ten games out of first place one month into the season as usual, the Blackhawks' playoff run was filling bars and clubs every third night

Chicago experiences all four seasons. And we embrace all of them, each with its own magnificent splendor. But summer is the crown jewel, especially after a brutal, arctic winter. The slow arrival of spring did not temper the excitement that the worst of the weather was behind us. Our glowing metropolis explodes with life, festivals, boats, parties, outdoor concerts, and al fresco dining when the mercury begins to rise and the days grow longer. Summer in Chicago is one long party, starting on Memorial Day and ending on Labor Day.

It was the first Friday night in May and still coat weather, but Chicagoans were starting to emerge from their winter hibernation. The sky was gray and there was still a strong, crisp chill in the air, but I did not feel it thanks to my nervousness. This was the night I would release the beast from the trunk (the Uber paraphernalia I received last month when I registered to drive) and get baptized on the streets of laughter, fear, and shame.

Seven p.m. I drove to a local Starbucks parking lot for staging, plugging in all the apparatuses needed to start this saga. I came prepared and took inventory: an Uber iPhone, a GPS, an iPod, a can of Ozium (air disinfectant), plastic bags—for those who chose to share their evening of over indulgence with me in Hi Ho (my car), a journal for harvesting data, a pack of Marlboro Silver, and a cup of coffee. I adjusted the bulletproof back pad and strategically positioned the protection devices that my friend Joe had given me in the pouch on the driver's side door, as if I really need this stuff...what overkill! *Houston, we are ready for takeoff.*

Now what?

As the car began to roll, I realized the mission was at hand. I turned on the iPhone. The Uber interface came to life and asked me to log in with my username and password. I was so flustered I couldn't remember either. I pulled over and tried various iterations until I finally keyed my way in. There sat a black car icon, representing my car and me aimlessly wandering the city, on a grid of streets, making my birthplace foreign and confusing to me.

Apprehension seeped in, overcoming reason and distracting me. Do I drive, or do I sit in one location? I merged back into traffic with all the confidence of a newly-licensed driver. The world slowly started to rotate, reminding me of the beginning of a Tilt-a-Whirl ride—the only difference being that I was behind the wheel of an automobile in the third most congested city in the country. Fear, excitement, and panic consumed me. A pounding noise from the right rear fender of the car registered somewhere in my brain. A fixed-gear cyclist was punching my car with his fist.

Taking a deep breath, I gave the clown a one-finger salute. *So that's how it's going to be out here.* Was it time to get a bit more aggressive? I picked up my iPod, selected the Eagles' "In the City." *Let's have some fun.*

I had been behind the wheel for fifteen minutes, listening to the Eagles, and nothing had happened. Was there some other step I forgot about? A function overlooked that started the process? I continued nosing Hi Ho up and down streets, and then I heard a peculiar buzz. I wondered what it could be, and then I realized this was it and I had four seconds to touch the small iPhone screen to accept the fare. When I tapped the phone, a name, rating, and address appeared.

My insides quivered like a fresh bowl of Jell-O, while my thoughts frantically unscrambled what I should be doing next. I tried to punch the address into the GPS, but my fingers kept missing the correct numbers and letters. The guy behind me was honking, so I pulled over to the side of the rode to manipulate the GPS, avoiding a crater-sized pothole along the way. I stabbed the address into the system, only to realize that I was just one block away. Moments were wasted as I dwelled on feeling like a clueless idiot. Still, I followed the GPS directions to a T and they took me to Diversey Rock 'n' Bowl on the Chicago River. Standing in front of the bowling alley was a group of five twenty-something kids out having fun.

Three girls and two guys approached the car. I still didn't know if they were the fare. As soon as the car stopped, the rear door opened and a young lady with a loud voice said, "Patrick?" At that moment, Pat was introduced to Patrick. Pat, the businessman, fifty-something father of two, was introduced to "Patrick," the rideshare driver, the dude who ferried the young and the restless of Chicago in his Mercedes. Pat had no idea how complex this new relationship would become. I asked to see her driver's license, as the ten-minute rideshare tutorial had taught me. She looked at me as if I were senile. "Why?" I didn't even have the time to tell her that the entire group was not welcome in the car before all five people piled in like it was their mom's Country Squire station wagon headed to the local Dairy Queen on Sunday afternoon. I tried to tell them that the number of passengers allowed in the car was four. "Chill, dude. It's okay," they said, and blurted out the name of a bar on Lincoln Avenue.

I had a brief out-of-body experience. I was hovering over my car, observing strangers continuing to party and carry on. *There are strangers in my car,* I thought. *Holy shit!* I settled back into a focused driving mode and resumed pothole surfing, which occasionally shifted the car into the other lane of traffic or into the sacred bicycle lane to the right, and I started to realize the level of concentration required. Potholes able to immobilize a Patton tank, and aggressive cyclists in the lane to my right I was more or less used to, but add navigating five loud partiers to a specific destination, while merging street and screen realities, was a great deal to manage.

In close quarters, I realized that you can't help but overhear what is being said. "Megan, I never realized your ass was so boney," said a guy in the backseat, with the illegal fifth passenger on his lap. Then another girl blurted out gossip about two of the group's acquaintances who had "hooked up."

Though trying to stay focused on the road, something in my

periphery steered my vision further right. The young man in the passenger seat had put my prescription sunglasses on. "Dude, these are cool." I took a proverbial second glance and realized I'd better get a bit more aggressive in my actions and attitude or this experiment wouldn't work.

"Hey, junior, do you have three hundred bucks on you?"

"Hell no, dude. Why?"

"Because that is what the glasses cost. Take them off and put them back where you found them." His eyes definitely displayed a little shock and what I perceived to be a bit of fear.

I still had the Eagles playing at low volume and one of the debutantes in the backseat screamed, "'Take It to the Limit!' Crank this shit up."

At that point, I totally confused the guy next to me when I nodded at him and said, "What are you waiting for? Turn up the damn volume."

We finally arrived at the bar and they piled out. "Thanks, dude, for the great ride." I rated them on the iPhone (a 5). The fare was $7.85.

My first fare under my belt, I drove on, aimlessly poking around Wicker Park, Lakeview, Lincoln Park, Evanston, Hyde Park, and the various active areas of downtown Chicago. The iPhone would buzz and like a good trained seal I would pull over, plug the address into the GPS, and proceed to the next land of the unknown. I completed a few quick trips, nothing unique. I also learned about driving to an address and getting a cancelation. After taking the time to locate the address and drive to the site with the phone engaged to that fare and wasting gas, hearing a dead buzz tone, alerting me that the fare had canceled the request as I approached the target location, could really put me in a foul attitude. (Over the next few months, I would come to expect this about twice a night.) After the frustration and disappointment of this first cancelation wore off, I continued to drive and pick up short-distance, run-of-the-mill fares. I checked my notepad. After two hours, I was at about $40 in revenues.

It was getting close to nine p.m. and I was buzzed to one of the nicest streets in Lincoln Park. The fare had a female name. She would be responsible for the fare and her checking account would be debited. After I pulled up to the address, I noticed a couple walking out of a stunning contemporary townhouse. She had on a skin-tight pair of black leather pants and a sheer white blouse, her blond hair was extremely teased. He had on a sport coat and no tie, and his shirt was unbuttoned to just above his navel. Judging by the cut of his jacket, I was pretty sure that when he had purchased it, he had received three more free. Guys dressed like this crack me up. They gave me the address to the Publican restaurant located in the funky West Loop.

As I pulled away, the lady started digging in her evening bag. The man leaned over, "What are you looking for?"

She didn't answer, so he asked her again, and she said, "Never mind." He asked again and she said, "Really, it's not important."

We were now five blocks away from her townhouse and this verbal volley was getting irritating. I looked in the mirror and asked, "Do you want me to turn around so you can go back to the house and get your blow?"

She smiled, her face turned beet red, and she said, "You are so perceptive. Please, will you?" How did I know she was looking for a vial of cocaine, you might ask? Judging by the small size of her evening bag, I knew a tampon or pack of cigarettes would have consumed half the bag, and she was looking for something very small. Sometimes it pays to be an old and worldly guy who was a stockbroker in the eighties.

She got out and sashayed back to the townhouse with her date salivating at her behind, returning five minutes later. Her toned ass, clad in leather, squeaked as she slid back into the rear seat. Then they talked about what groceries she had bought for the next day, because he was spending the night at her place. They also partook in groping and kissing while he narrated, "So good, baby. So good." Give me a break. I was getting uncomfortable and embarrassed in my own vehicle. Little did I know this behavior would seem tame to me in a few short weeks.

She gushed about the proteins they would eat and the limited carbs they wouldn't consume, and so on. Then, out of the clear blue, this guy (who was way out of his league) said to me, "Hey, driver. Tell her she has a hot ass." I didn't say anything and realized that I was quite taken aback because that was the first time anybody had ever called me "driver." He said again, a bit louder this time, "Hey, driver. Tell her she has a hot ass."

I smiled and nodded. "I really do not wish to go there." During this verbal exchange, Lou Reed's "Walk on the Wild Side" was playing on the radio. *How perfect,* I thought. He was badgering me the same way he had been obnoxiously probing her about what she was rummaging for in her evening bag.

The obstinate pig shouted at me this time, "Hey, driver. Tell her she has a hot ass!" He was relentless in his quest for this asinine compliment.

I looked in the mirror. "Hey, buddy. Why is it so important that I tell her she has a hot ass?" He replied that she was going to her fortieth birthday party, and every guy there was going to tell her she had a hot ass and that he wanted her to get used to hearing it. I looked in the rearview mirror at this overweight king of online dating and asked sarcastically, "Really?" I smiled and nodded.

Finally, I arrived at the location. Sneezy and Sleazy were ready to parade her hot bottom around the restaurant's dining room. As she got out of the car in her black leather pants, Sneezy turned, looked at me, and then winked. I smiled and nodded. Driving away, a coy grin appeared on my face as my old ego got a boost and Patrick thought, *Maybe this old boy still has some game left in him.*

So I resumed the routine of picking up young people and transporting them to various nightspots around town. In two hours, I had gone to Wicker Park from Old Town and back several times. Hi Ho was wearing a path on pothole-ridden North Avenue. Every time I hit Wicker Park, I was amazed at the number of young people spilling onto the streets. A whole new world of tattooed people in extreme dress resided at the intersection of North and Damen Avenues. The crawling traffic had to navigate around all the rideshare cars and taxis idling with their flashers on, as they waited for fares. Bright lights, one bar after another, street actors, punks, thugs, competing doughnut shops, and taco stands were everywhere. This is as close as Chicago gets to a cross between Venice Beach, California, and SoHo in New York City. The streets were electric with energy, and I would soon find out that this pace would not stop until dawn.

As I slowly trawled the main drag of Wicker Park, a shiny silver object caught my eye. It was a chrome circle roughly six feet in diameter, with a man sporting a silver tinsel wig sitting on a silver bicycle within the circle. Later, I found out from a passenger that for two dollars this guy would ride the inner arc of the chrome circle. *What a wild area,* I thought, as I waited for the phone's next buzz.

My wait was short, and I quickly programmed the GPS. I was off to the side streets of an area known as Ukrainian Village. Some homes were festooned with blue and gold flags demonstrating expatriate loyalty to the homeland, which was facing increasing pressures from Vladimir Putin. I arrived at a three-story brownstone apartment building and waited for Chuck, who, the phone told me, had a rating of 4.6.

Chuck and another young man approached the car and got in. Chuck appeared to be like any other male passenger in his early twenties, but his buddy seemed a bit preppy for the neighborhood. He wore Mr. Peabody horn-rimmed glasses, a Tattersall oxford shirt, and khaki pants. Chuck informed me that we were headed to an area I really don't care for located west of Wicker Park on Milwaukee Avenue. The next thing I knew, Peabody asked me, "Aren't you ashamed of what you're doing?" I didn't say a word, but looked in the rearview mirror, smiling and nodding. The young man followed that question with, "What? Does your Mercedes need gas?" in a very sarcastic tone. I could see that Chuck was getting very uneasy with his friend's goading. I did not say a word. I decided to just get this little jerk to his destination, and then I could not believe what I heard next: "My generation is going to define your future." This brat was the walking definition of hubris.

At that point, Patrick hit the lock button on the driver's door, which locks all the doors, and asked, "Junior, why don't I define the next two hours of your future and drop your smart ass off at 55th and State Streets?" This would not be a good neighborhood to be sporting the Mr. Peabody look on the first warm Saturday night of the season.

He fired back angrily, "I'm going to give you a bad rating."

Patrick pulled over on the spot and said, "Get the fuck out of my car." This would be the first of a long line of "Get the fuck out of my car" commands that Patrick would deliver over the next three months.

Poor Chuck looked like he was going to soil himself. As he sheepishly left the car, he looked us if his rideshare future had vanished before his eyes, thanks to his buddy's arrogant mouth. I gave Chuck a good rating and shut the phone off until my blood pressure came down. I put The Who's classic tune "My Generation" on and headed back to the Gold Coast. As he drove, Pat thought of the elderly man in the tan golf jacket and tweed hat that had caught his attention the day he had picked up his rideshare iPhone. Pat wondered how he was faring on the streets with the likes of Peabody looming out there.

I returned to picking up tired, standard-issue riders who just wanted to get home after a night of eating, drinking, and loud talking. Entering the last hour of the day, I decided to forge on for three more hours into the new morning. Little did I know that between midnight and two a.m., the craziness of the witching hours would unfold before my bloodshot eyes. While I waited in front of crowded bars with young people pouring into the streets, I became aware of the number of other four-door sedans with their flashers on waiting alongside the traditional taxicabs. I then realized the financial magnitude of jockeying the over-served to and fro and that it is a major industry in this city. The sexy-miniskirted, perfectly primped young ladies of the early evening were returning with running makeup, disheveled dress, and rankness from hanging out in hot crowded bars.

Already I was beginning to get the hang of the Uber phone, the GPS, and how to crack off a good U-turn on a crowded urban street. Checking my account, I couldn't believe I had made only $150. Also, I realized my tailbone was killing me, my sciatic nerve was twitching, and my fifty-year-plus bladder needed to be relieved—now I understood why late-night doughnut shops are so popular amongst the taxi and livery set. I decided to take a much-needed break and stopped at a twenty-four-hour doughnut shop, but before I pulled in, I hid all clues that I was a rideshare driver. The last thing I wanted to do in the middle of the night was upset a group of legitimate taxi drivers.

I waited in line for the men's room, trying to pass myself off as a normal guy who just had to relieve himself, not a bastard scab brother of the taxi trade. On the way out, I got a cup a coffee for the final two-hour thrust and returned to the car to stretch my sore back and throbbing legs. I got in and fired up my iPod, selecting Jackson

Browne's "Boulevard." Feeling a newfound rush of energy, I continued to push steel into the early hours of a new day through the unforgiving streets of Chicago.

Right away the phone began to buzz and the parade of the inebriated carried on, from solo fares to groups as large as five. I was bouncing from Wicker Park to Evanston and back to Hyde Park. I felt efficiencies starting to develop in how I was dealing with this stressful task—yes, stressful. Driving for yourself, your family, or your friends is a totally different experience than driving for strangers. They had chosen this method of transportation because they loved the technology and the fact that it was a seamless transaction (no cash, just a debit to their checking account). Their safekeeping was placed in my hands through the wizards of coding. Then there's the state of the roads, the drunken jaywalkers, the bicyclists, the police, and finally, the dodging of drunk drivers in the late hours.

But I was beginning to feel like I knew what I was doing. The conversations were plentiful. I was hearing about careers, romances, colleges, and any other topic you could think of. I didn't realize that in a few weeks, when my driving confidence would be really developed, I would hear about topics I could never imagine on day one. The intimate confines of my car would be transformed into part confessional, part exhibition stage.

The iPhone sported a new red banner I hadn't seen before, and certain areas of the map on the application were highlighted in pink. It was surge price time. The demand was so high that the company had added a surcharge on fares. I had no idea then how high fares could climb when the system was bleeding red with demanding riders needing to get home. "Wow. The bonus round," I said to myself, and got another burst of energy.

The pace was brisk for a little more than an hour. Hi Ho had developed a stench from all the sweaty people getting in and out of its backseat, and I realized that the can of Ozium had been a damn good idea. The drunkenness of the fares grew worse as the late night turned to early morning and the bars began to close. I noticed that some of the people in one group of five were a mild shade of green and were taking deep breaths to refrain from regurgitating. The thought of the one on the lap of the person directly behind me being one bad pothole away from dropping her evening of fun down the back of my neck was not pleasant. Fortunately, the young lady in question was able to hold her cookies and I arrived at the destination dry and stench-free. I turned to watch the four young, miniskirt-clad women and one guy in high-top Converse shoes get out of the car, and I came to two realizations: (1) Stocks in companies that sell female underwear should be shorted on Monday because sales of undergarments must be atrocious, and (2) somewhere between 1985 and now, pubic hair had become an option.

Pulling a U-turn, I headed back downtown listening to Leo Sayer's "Long Tall Glasses." No sooner had I hit Wells Street than the phone buzzed. It was two a.m., but what the hell! What was one more drunken passenger? I picked up a chubby white couple and they gave me an address in Humboldt Park. *Joy*, I thought. Not the type of neighborhood I want to go to at this time of night. We began to roll, and I started to hear a loud slurping noise. They were kissing, or at least trying to. This was a loud, wet, glugging noise that made the hair on my neck stand up and made me pray to hear long, jagged fingernails being dragged across a chalkboard.

The woman whispered, "John, we're making out in a Mercedes." At this time of the morning, I truly was in no mood to be captain of the rolling love boat.

Repulsion picked up as I looked in the rearview mirror and

thought, *Get some technique, you bumbling clown*. The three-mile drive seemed like it would never end. I felt like I had two Saint Bernards in the backseat that hadn't had a drop of water in a week.

Finally we were on the side street where they lived. The potholes were like craters, and I thought about the roadways of Iraq. Hi Ho was listing back and forth like a ship in a bad storm, and the obnoxious noises continued. We arrived at their apartment building and the love serpents got out. Enough for one night, I decided, and I headed home, trying to shake off my newfound repulsion for slurping.

About three miles from home I decided to take it easy and not rush. I couldn't help but notice how many homeless people took shelter under the viaducts late at night, their shopping carts filled with all their worldly goods unsafely resting next to them. "How do they sleep out here?" I asked myself. As I took Hi Ho slowly up North Avenue, I glimpsed what I thought was a rabbit crossing the road. Getting closer, I realized it was no rabbit, but a rat. Nice. Vermin lived fifty feet from that guy's master suite under the viaduct. I locked on to the thought that this shouldn't be happening in a country as rich as ours. I took note too of the late-night diners and taco joints, most of which were crowded with groups of people who would soon become a fascination for me. They were all the people of the streets.

The car was bringing me home. My maiden voyage was over and this evening of challenges had grossed $250. As I pulled into the driveway, the Edwin Hawkins Singers were reveling in "Oh Happy Day." I found it difficult to unwind after my first night of driving. I went to my second-floor balcony and looked at the stars. I live in a townhouse in the heart of the city on the west bank of the Chicago River. During the summer months I almost feel as if I'm out in the country—until I spy the top of the Hancock Center antennas above the trees. It has always been my place for meditation and reflection. Little did I know that this early morning exercise would repeat itself quite often over the next twelve weeks. That night I laughed about the concept of "Patrick" and was excited about all that was to come.

On Saturday morning, I didn't wake up until eleven. When I stood up, I couldn't believe how stiff the right side of my back and my right knee were. Damn, I hurt. I went to the computer and made my entries from the data I gathered the previous night into carefully-crafted spreadsheets. I was still processing the fact that I had transported a full night of strangers in *my car.* People had made out and fondled each other, again, in *my car.* I had almost received a vomit bath, again, in *my car.*

Checking my online profile, I saw all my fares and all my ratings. I became incensed that I was rated a 4.8, not a 5.0, and I wondered who had lowballed me—as if this really mattered—but then I realized it was Mr. Peabody, the little preppy bastard. Anyway, I was over it, because in a perverse way, I couldn't wait the few hours till Saturday night to witness the citywide party again.

The better part of the day was spent healing my aches and pains and thinking of how to improve my driving performance. I also contemplated how to put myself in a position to capture rich data for my article. But concentration on that was quickly lost, and the next thought I had was to put more plastic bags in the pouches on the back of the seat. "A truly deep and strategic thought," I voiced to myself. I planned my attack for the upcoming evening by strategizing the best locations for capturing quality fares. I decided to leave home at six p.m.

I chewed aspirin for my leg and back while getting the car cleaned at the neighborhood hand car wash. The rideshare company wanted us drivers to always present a sparkling car. How noble of them. As I walked to my freshly tidied car, the guy who had cleaned the inside said, "Sir, wait." He approached me timidly and said, "I have something from the backseat of your car."

Now what? I thought. *Did somebody leave a pair of panties in my car?* Then I realized that couldn't be it because from what I could gather, none of my female passengers had worn any.

He opened his hand. In it were two tightly rolled joints. I smiled, laughed, and said, "You can hang on to them." He smiled, and I left. I drove away, chuckling at the juxtaposition of my traditional day life and my newfound evening activities. As time went on, the extent of the tension of this juxtaposition would eventually creep into every aspect of my life.

Saturday night and I was back on the road. A few minutes before six, I began my external transformation from Pat, the old businessman, to Patrick, the rideshare dude. The neighborhood Starbucks became to me what the phone booth was to Clark Kent. Not only was I a chameleon in the way I dressed, I was also morphing into one in my head. "Brown Sugar" by the Rolling Stones was my opening soundtrack for day two, another warm early spring night. It was Saturday night, date night, the night single lads prowl and hunt while the little ladies dress to the nines to cast their baited hooks, and I would be providing the transportation for this centuries-old ritual.

I decided to start my drive on Belmont, one of the more colorful streets in the city. Quickly, I was buzzed and diverted to a side street. Four people who seemed to be in their late thirties appeared outside the car. To my surprise, the ladies had long dresses on and the men had donned suits. They carried two tastefully wrapped big boxes and were fidgeting about the seating arrangement. The women and one man got in the backseat with the boxes. They were all big people, so tall that their knees were forcing their arms into their fleshy chins. The other man sat in the front passenger seat, but he couldn't get the seat back for enough legroom because of the height and substantial girth of the person behind him. This poor guy was very uncomfortable, the picture of total discomfort, his face beet red because of the tight tie around his thick neck, and it showed. He was not accustomed to wearing a suit. That is a sixth sense you get about a person when you wear a suit every day for thirty years. Weirdly, the group treated me with an aura of professionalism, in the same manner that one would treat a limousine driver. They were in deep philosophical discussion about the wedding they were going to attend.

For shits and giggles, I interjected, "Is the temperature comfortable for the ladies?" I apologized for the potholes, as if I could do anything about them. We were headed to the Drake Hotel off of Michigan Avenue, so I had to take Lake Shore Drive. Two exits before Michigan Avenue, traffic came to a standstill. The women started to get concerned about being late for the ceremony. Looking to the right, I saw Tiny in the passenger seat looking like he wanted to cry. I turned to him. "Why don't you step out and take off the suit coat and loosen the tie? We aren't going anywhere for a while." I casually put on "Ninety-Six Tears" by Question Mark and the Mysterians as we began the long, agonizing wait. After thirty minutes of waiting in traffic, I dropped them off, and damn, a $28 fare right out of the box. I watched the four large people hustle through the Drake's revolving doors to see someone's nuptials.

Quickly I left the Loop, trying to escape the brutal early evening traffic, and headed up Division Street. Soon I was directed to Lakeview to pick up a fare. A young man in a sport coat and a tie appeared at the car door. This seemingly ordinary passenger would force me to realize one of my worst fears on only my second night of driving. He asked if I could take him to a certain private club downtown where I have held a membership for over three decades. The doormen know my car, and they rush to park it every time I arrive. *What the hell am I going to do?* I thought. He then asked me if I had ever been there and wondered how

16

the food was. He was going to a company-sponsored event and it was his first time there. Dumbfounded, I stayed mute. I pulled over at the corner about half a block from the club entrance and told him it would save him time and money if he hoofed it the last half block. He was amenable and left the car. I sat in the car on the side of the street and gazed out the window in disbelief, pondering the statistical probability of this destination request so early on in my experiment. I drove away listening to Ringo Starr's "It Don't Come Easy."

The city had waited eight nasty months for this type of weather, and everybody was out. I was getting buzzed nonstop, picking up couples and getting them to restaurants all over the city. I began to notice that a nice byproduct of this gig was that I was getting turned on to good new places to eat and fun places to go. Pat was also envious that he was not enjoying a fun Saturday night.

By now I felt like one of Pavlov's dogs as I was buzzed to an apartment building on the Gold Coast, where I picked up a young couple. She was dripping in a spring gray Chanel suit and toting a large Prada bag. He was just as expensively and nattily attired as his female counterpart. They directed me to a Near North tapas restaurant on North Avenue. Her phone rang and she turned to her partner and told him it was Daddy.

"Hello, Daddy. How are you?...I have such big news!" she screamed, without moving her teeth. "Daddy, the foundation I work for has chosen me to give a presentation to Mr. George Soros. Do you know who he is, Daddy?"

Okay, I thought. *Rule number one: I am Patrick, the rideshare driver, not Pat, the businessman, and I have no opinions political or otherwise.*

"Daddy, he is some kind of philanthropic hedge fund trader, and he has this wonderful vision for a New World Order!"

Aren't we all lucky? I thought. I wondered if she would look as good in gray burlap as she did in gray silk Chanel. As the father and daughter continued to chat, I understood her excitement. Hell, the only cooler thing would be presenting to the Koch brothers. Heh heh. Just a joke. When they were out of the car, I unclenched my molars and got ready for my next fare.

The evening was running very smoothly. I could feel the dinner rush ending, and no one had asked me to tell his girlfriend that she had a hot ass. *Now that is progress*, I thought. The earlier near miss at the city club still had me a bit uneasy. The pace of passengers started to slow around nine p.m.

I was buzzed to DePaul University and waited outside a dormitory. Two young girls approached the car in the shortest skirts I had ever seen. Their hair and makeup were perfect. They asked me to take them to a nightclub in the West Loop, and while I delivered them to their destination, they chatted about the upcoming evening. They were both hoping to hook up. As one expressed her wishes for her future unknown partner to be hairless, I almost ran a red light.

I was invisible to these two girls, no different than the car's transmission. They were going into graphic detail about what they were going to do and what they wanted done to themselves. I was speechless, which is difficult for me and rare. I was old enough to be their father, yet not one bit of shame or restraint was coming from the backseat. A shrinking violet I am not, but the discussion bordered on the lewd and pornographic. Patrick was grooving on every detail of the sordid conversation, while Pat was a bit more uncomfortable. I had no idea that in a few weeks this ride would seem tame—nothing out of the ordinary for a Saturday night.

After dropping the girls off, I put on some music by Genesis and waited for the buzz. Next thing I knew I was picking up a couple in their early thirties from a neighborhood tavern. He was a big, burly white guy with a beard. She was a very pleasant, small Asian woman, dwarfed by his strong presence. He asked me if I could turn up the music. I said sure. This guy went on an excited rant about Genesis and how he loved their music and when he had last seen them in concert. Over their twenty-minute ride, I had a nice conversation with a stranger about music. To my surprise, he added a comment to his rating of me: *Patrick is the coolest driver and has the best music.* This quote appeared on my weekly tracking report. When I read it, I said to myself, "This Patrick sounds like a cool guy. I'll have to hang out with him someday."

The night continued. Old Town. Wicker Park. Gold Coast. West Loop. Logan Square. Logan Square was a new neighborhood for me. *What fantastic vintage homes, truly a beautiful neighborhood,* I thought as I enjoyed one stunning graystone after another. The square itself is just as much a pain in the ass to drive as Randolph Street, with the inner one-way streets that run parallel with the main drag, but it was a nice place nonetheless. I figured out that if I came out on a certain street, I was on the main drag off Milwaukee Avenue near the grunge bars.

The next address was to a bar west of Milwaukee, and to my surprise, three people over the age of sixty got in the car. I had to ask, "What the hell are you doing around this neighborhood?" They were in town for a graduation and had heard that the bar they had just left was known for good blues bands. They asked to be taken to a hotel in the Loop. They were from Portland, Oregon, and were very nice people. Being prone to Midwestern stereotypes, I figured they were old hippies. Before I knew it, one of the guys went on a rant about the mayor of Chicago and the crowd the mayor came from in Washington. This fellow was a Tea Party member who lived in Portland, liked the blues, and was to the right of right. "I am so confused," Pat said to Patrick. I dropped them off and listened to "Franklin's Tower" by the Grateful Dead.

What a peculiar night. What a diverse ten square miles. I chuckled as I downed another cup of coffee. From the New World Order to the Tea Party. It was time to stretch my back and relieve myself. I realized I'd better vary my doughnut shop stops so the taxi guys wouldn't catch on to my clandestine employment. It was ten o'clock in the evening, and the bar traffic would start to get heavy soon. While on my break, I realized for the first time how isolated and vulnerable I felt on the streets of my hometown, when my car had just emptied, leaving me in a neighborhood that I would have never known if I didn't drive Uber.

My goal was to go at it until three a.m., so I knew I'd better pace myself. A buzz came from a watering hole in the West Loop, where five people got in. They asked a question that I would be asked at least four hundred more times: "Hey, Patrick. What's with the car? This is the nicest Uber car we've ever had!"

I was still nervous every time I picked up a new fare, and I still fumbled a bit with the GPS. A few times I even forgot to hit the begin ride function on the iPhone and gave a few lucky passengers free rides. I can't stress enough the amount of positive and negative mental stimulation that I experienced while performing this task. Driving seems simple, yet an eight-hour shift takes a toll on your car, body, and mind. Soon, however, I would find out that the more relaxed I appeared, the more engaging most passengers would become.

The evening was moving along at a quick pace. At eleven forty-five, I was either taking people out to bars to start their evening or nursing them home after several hours of fun. I observed that the young people wore a few uniforms. The women, for instance, were in either black mini-dresses or black stretch pants. The number of tight black stretch pants getting in and out of my car often made me feel like a dromedary podiatrist, but it was the fashion of the day, and who was I to complain? The young men always seemed to be underdressed, usually wearing jeans, T-shirts, untucked and un-pressed button-down Oxford shirts, and athletic shoes. It was explained to me by one young lady that the women dress more to outdo other women than to impress the men. *Damn, I'm getting old,* I thought after hearing that logic, but she was probably correct in her observation.

An address appeared on the iPhone and quickly I regained my driver focus. Five attractive early-twenty-something girls entered the car in Bucktown, another funky, trendy area. They immediately started talking about drugs, mainly marijuana. For all they knew I could have been an off-duty Chicago cop picking up some extra scratch. They were feeling no pain, and the cute little blond in the passenger seat turned to me and said, "There should be rideshare J."

"Rideshare J?" I replied quizzically.

"Yes, the drivers should be able to sell weed to the riders."

I looked at her and smiled. *Great idea for Denver,* I thought. The conversation throughout the car critiqued all the fashionable illegal drugs available at a dealer near you. I don't know what possessed me, but I turned to my new friend in the front passenger seat and Patrick said, "I am Walter White's age."

She got a smile from ear to ear and screamed, "He was the coolest dude!" Walter White is the meth-dealing former high school teacher in the successful television series *Breaking Bad*. This "cool dude" she was referring to was responsible for the deaths of at least two hundred people and the ruination of his family in the show.

Cool? Pat thought. *Maybe I missed something when I watched the program.* They were a friendly group and told Patrick he was the coolest Uber driver they'd ever had. I drove away listening to J.J. Cale's "Cocaine."

The pace didn't stop. I watched one group of tanked, sweaty kids after another crawl in and out of my car, looking for the next experience in their quest for excitement. They seemed to blend into one another. Very little differentiates drunk and loud people from one another in the middle of the night.

Late-night couples make an interesting fare. They end up going home together, making two stops, or negotiating the yes or no of making one stop. The latter usually provided the best entertainment to me, commander of their coach to either bliss or angst. "I will make you breakfast." "I can't. My fish need to be fed." "It's a bad time of the month" (a proven showstopper). "I have company staying with me, and I have to be up early for church" (another good stop sign). And finally, the blunt, "You're a jerk. Thanks for the free booze and the ride." There were nights I'd listen to these verbal volleys and wonder why I'd ever need television again when I had a front-row seat for the rawest of all reality entertainment. My favorite outcome of these situations was when the guy got dropped off first and the girl said to me, "You know that address he gave you to drop me off at when we got in the car? Change that and take me to this club or bar." Ouch. That can create trust issues for even an old Uber driver like me. Off to the new address we would go.

Saturday night continued to employ me as a bar-to-home shuttle and I stayed reasonably cool, with nothing out of the ordinary happening. Things were going relatively smoothly, considering I was a novice driver. Then I was buzzed to a strange address. I forged on, but the next thing I knew, I was in a deserted industrial park on the Chicago River. It was dark, not a soul in sight, and I was waiting in front of an industrial garage door surrounded by discarded tires and scrap iron. The door went up, and a tall, ominous figure dressed all in black emerged from the pitch-dark garage. He got into the car and gave me, in a dull, soft voice, an address on the Southwest Side of the city.

It was after one-thirty in the morning, and I was not feeling too good about this situation. To make this even creepier, he sat in the seat directly behind the driver's seat. My mind flashed to the scene in *The Godfather* where the guy in the driver's seat is strangled with a piano wire by the thug sitting behind him. My legs kicking through the windshield was not what I had envisioned for me or Hi Ho. *Damn,* I thought. *Ten years of taking cholesterol medicine to end up like this. Oh shit.* I slowly reached for the Taser and placed it between my legs. Carefully, I turned it to the on position for the first time.

The ride was silent. This guy breathed loudly and looked like Steven Seagal with pockmarks. I heard every crack in the road, and my heart skipped a beat as the car absorbed deep potholes. From my subconscious I kept hearing, *Don't forget the cannoli.*

We finally arrived at the address he had given me, a place just as unnerving as the dump where I had picked him up. He didn't say a word, not thank you or anything. He just got out and walked into another pitch-dark building. I drove away slowly and said to myself, "Why do I feel that someday I will read something grotesque about this guy in the papers?"

Newly emerged from the side street where I had left my comforting friend, I realized that I was in an unsavory neighborhood. My preoccupation with not getting strangled hadn't allowed for any thought about where I was headed. Damn, this was not good. Pat immediately turned off the iPhone because there was no way he was picking anybody up in this shithole of a neighborhood at two in the morning on a hot, muggy night. Patrick developed a new survival plan to get home, which was simple: Run every red light. *Hell, give me a ticket,* he thought. *At least I would have a partial police escort out of this septic tank.* Pat was freaking out. There was a strong and evident police presence, but they were consumed by more daunting challenges. He couldn't believe how many people were out at this time of morning.

What I didn't realize was that I would experience this uncomfortable feeling again, on a more profound trip with a gruesome outcome. I was driving at a fast clip for a city street, but I still couldn't help noticing the streetwalkers leaning against the cars, and what appeared to be drug deals going down in the deserted parking lots under the sneakers roped over phone lines. Oh, how I missed wild and wasted kids stumbling into my car from the Near North bars. At that point, it sunk in that my escapades on the street weren't going to be all party shuttle and romantic rent-a-coach.

It was well after two in the morning. I had vowed that I would drive until after three. I was then called to Hubbard Street, which was still overflowing with people getting crazy. I picked up two ladies and two men, and, like most late night fares, they were feeling no pain. They told me there would be three stops: two in Evanston and one in Deerfield. Evanston is the suburb immediately north of Chicago and Deerfield is substantially north of Evanston. We proceeded to Lake Shore Drive and began to travel up the lakefront. They were having fun, but were by no means obnoxious. They were classmates in an MBA program at Northwestern University and were celebrating their completion of the first year of the program.

The fella in the front seat noticed I had a school ring on and was able to make out the three initials engraved on it: *MBA*. He asked me, "What's up? The car, the MBA ring, and you're an Uber driver at three in the morning?" I smiled and came clean about the research paper I was planning to write based on this experience. They asked about other works I had written, and we started talking about business. I dropped the two ladies and one guy off in Evanston and was left with the business-curious guy in the front seat. We discussed the capital markets, private equity, managerial styles, and what avenues I would pursue if I were entering the business world with an MBA a year from then. We arrived at his home and I turned off the iPhone, which had a nice fare of $28 flashing on it. We continued to talk for at least ninety minutes. He was a veteran of the war in Afghanistan, married, two children, and excited about completing his graduate degree.

The sky was getting lighter and the birds were chirping, and I headed back home to the city. *What a night, especially the end,* I thought. I had gone from the terror of the ghetto to the serenity and safety of the North Shore. My evening had gone from driving a menacing stranger in the dark to talking to an outgoing vet who had such bold dreams for himself and his family's future that he couldn't contain them. I also laughed that I was transforming myself into "Patrick," a blue-collar service employee. As I approached my driveway, I was listening to Roger Miller's classic musical tale of the life of a down-and-out drifter, "King of the Road."

The next day, I woke in the early afternoon. As I hobbled down the stairs to the kitchen, I remembered every stop sign that had forced me to put pressure on my right leg, which was now shooting pain up to my lower back. I wondered how many rideshare drivers were over fifty.

Those old-man thoughts left my sordid brain as I rehashed the events of the previous evening. I began to enter the statistical data I had gathered the night before in my spreadsheet. I kept turning over in my head what was happening in my car and couldn't wait to share the crazy tales with a few of my close friends. Then, with only two days of driving under my belt, it hit me. Scrap the research paper. There's a book on those streets. Taking up my pen, I recorded the events of my first Saturday night of being Patrick, the Uber dude. I paused several times to either laugh or scratch my head, with a sigh. Quantifiable graphs were to be replaced by certifiable graft.

I sat back and realized that I had been altered in just forty-eight hours. I had gone from being a traditional, conservative fifty-plus-year-old man to embracing a cast-my-fate-to-the-wind urban free spirit. I smiled about the dark alley and the ominous figure in my car. I craved overhearing provocative conversations about drugs and intimacies. I reveled in the mystery and unknown destinations waiting in the nights before me. I was an explorer with no set destination, in one of the most dangerous cities in the country, and I wanted to confront every aspect of risk. I was in the infancy of a deep and scary transformation. The perverse aspect of my thought process was that I could not wait until the next weekend to do this again.

PINK MUSTACHES

My first awareness of this new world came in the form of those pink mustaches affixed to the front grilles of cars. Were they a statement of support for those suffering from lip cancer? A friend told me they marked ridesharing vehicles. Then she educated me about this new disruptive business model infiltrating major cities all over the world. Then I was hearing strange new names in the business news: Uber, Lyft. The phenomenon was rampant among young people living in densely populated urban areas and seeking inexpensive transportation alternatives. Because I am a student of business and a strategic business consultant by trade, my curiosity was piqued. I decided to follow my intuition and explore this new sharing economy. My investigation of this new industry led me to the startling experiences that I now share.

I learned about the process of driving rideshare. I needed to know more about the most commonly used disruptive industry. I quickly understood that the only way to fundamentally understand this new business revolution was to become a participant.

Let me get this straight. *I have to subject myself to a background check and send in pictures of my driver's license, my car insurance, my car, and myself without interacting with one human being?* Hell, I continued to question the wisdom of this dump of data, but soon acknowledged to myself that the NSA most likely already had this information. Oh shit—no risk, no reward. The requested information was sent off to Uber.

During the next three days, I nervously looked at the company website and checked my status. Finally, after a week, an e-mail arrived informing me that I was cleared to drive . . . only after I had completed a ten-minute online training program and gone to the Uber corporate office to pick up the supplies needed for this venture. The training program was in no way enlightening and a true waste of time, but I completed it. The key elements stressed by the training were to always ask to see a piece of identification before the passenger entered the vehicle and to never allow more than four passengers into the vehicle at one time.

The next thing I knew, I was granted an access code to my personal account on the Web-based portal that would track the information regarding my fares, ratings, and weekly pay. There it all was: my picture, my license plate number, and my name, Patrick. I have always gone by Pat, but for the next three months, I would be Patrick or "Dude." Yes, I said ratings. The passengers are required to rate Patrick on a scale of one to five, five being the best. Patrick had to do the same for the passengers who briefly employed him and his automobile. I was entering the new democratized capitalism, the disruptive world of the sharing economy: ridesharing, VRBOs, renting out couch space, car rental by the hour, and one-way bicycle rental. This world was so foreign to me that I quickly checked my arms for a rash. And then I pictured a bitchin' tattoo on my right bicep. "Easy, tiger," I said to myself. "You were born in the middle of last century, not the beginning of this one."

After two weeks of internal debate and one failed attempt (I got there and chickened out), I arrived at the Uber offices in the trendy West Loop. (Where else?) *I'm really going through with this*. I climbed the stairs of the quaint, repurposed loft structure and was quickly overcome with the pleasant musk of stagnant old-building mold. I realized that this building was part of the historic Chicago meatpacking district, and I felt like I was about to be butchered.

I walked into the waiting area, which had lovely blue plastic chairs with chrome backing and legs. The chairs were arranged in a typical classroom format, and I settled in like I was at the DMV. Examining the room more closely, my perceptions changed. It was less DMV waiting room and more inmate visitors' area in the movie *Goodfellas*—except no one was performing oral sex five feet from the family visiting at the next table. I was a total emotional mess, and I almost turned around and left. Too late. I was given a number and asked to take a seat and wait. As I scanned the room, it was apparent to me that I was not the typical driving candidate.

There was a heavyset woman in her forties in tight jeans with an exaggerated camel toe (refer to the *Urban Dictionary* online, you will not find this defined in the *Readers Digest* glossary of terms) and a low-cut sweater, with the word *heaven* tattooed across her deep cleavage. An Uber employee was grilling her about allegations that she was soliciting riders for other services. *Interesting, entrepreneurial multitasking*, I thought. I guessed that several of her rides had happy endings.

My eyes wandered to a table where a young man from Uber was trying to communicate with an elderly gentleman who obviously had no clue what the company representative was trying to explain to him. The twenty-something was trying to tell him he was being forcibly retired by the company, and he was speaking loudly, slowly, and deliberately to this balding man with nostril hair to rival the wings of an eagle. I watched and heard the employee say, "Your rating is below one, and you don't know where you are going. Your customers are upset, and you cannot drive anymore."

The old man grunted, in some accent I couldn't place, "No, me drive." My mind flashed back to the early days of *Saturday Night Live*, and I could see the scene being played out, but instead of "No fries, cheeps," I heard, "No, me drive." This went on for twenty minutes, and finally, a tug-of-war ensued for the man's one-application iPhone that had been supplied by the firm. The company rep won the battle. I was really starting to debate my presence in this room. I tried thinking of ways to get out. I walked over to the window, but damn, I was on the fourth floor.

My wait continued for an additional twenty minutes, and I couldn't help taking inventory of the room. As I surveyed this foreign world, a young, plump couple sat down next to me. I was amazed at how every finger on the lady's hand had a ring so tight that a hacksaw would be needed to get any one of them off. She sported a nylon jacket boasting of her beer league softball team and tight black yoga pants. The couple turned two chairs in front of them around and prepared to feast on Taco Bell.

As I pretended to act interested and excited about being there, the woman asked me if I was there to be a driver. I smiled and nodded, not realizing that smiling and nodding would soon become my new defense mechanism and my silent way of saying, "Go fuck yourself."

She told me that she had been a driver for two months, knocking down serious cash, and that her boyfriend was going to drive as well. She turned to her boyfriend and grilled him with questions. "Did you bring your insurance card? Do you have your driver's license?" She made an attempt to cross her legs in an authoritative manner, straining the inseams of her ever-fashionable spandex pants.

With taco juice and lettuce on his face, he eased her concerns. I smiled and nodded. He wiped the hot sauce off his hand onto his black polyester pants and extended his hand to shake mine. I shook his hand, which had homemade tattoos that spelled *death* across his knuckles. I smiled and nodded. I also noticed that on the sleeve of his sport coat, the designer labels were still tacked in place. I wondered if that was a new fashion statement similar to keeping the holograph label on baseball caps. Again, I smiled and nodded.

I continued to wait, and this animated rideshare neighbor of mine continued to enjoy her crunchy cuisine and destroy a thirty-two-ounce Mountain Dew. Fully absorbing this culinary debacle, for a brief second I thought that New York's former Mayor Bloomberg might have been right. (Bloomberg had tried to limit the size of sugar-laden soft drinks that New York City consumers could purchase in an attempt to stave off obesity.) My conservative narrow-mindedness and love of liberty kicked back in in short order, and I smiled and nodded.

The line was moving slowly, and I was becoming impatient and increasingly uneasy. Eagle Nose had been removed, and the same young employee was arguing with another driver about whose liability it is when the company-issued iPhone gets dropped in a puddle. This took ten minutes, and the driver conceded that his next two hundred dollars of fares would go toward his new phone, allowing him to continue as a driver.

The room encompassed a vast demographic range, from the extremely elderly to young, new immigrants. I noticed one gentleman, well over seventy years of age, wearing a crisp beige golf jacket, a tweed cap, and an aura of properness and pride. He seemed nervous, as if he were waiting for test results in a doctor's office. My mind raced as I stared at him. *What did he do for a living for the better part of his life? Is he married or possibly a widower? Does he have grandchildren?* These thoughts and curiosities ran amuck inside my head. In the moment I couldn't have known how many times I'd think of him over the next few months, whenever I encountered a challenging or dangerous situation on the road.

Ridesharing is one of the last bastions of raw entrepreneurial capitalism. If an individual already owns a late-model four-door car, he or she can have a business. No licensing or franchising fees are needed; the only working capital required for the first week is the cost of a tank of gas. This concept gave me a weird Wild West type of feeling. Before us was an endeavor filled with uncertainty, risk, reward, and economic advancement for those brave enough to drive others. You don't even need a special driver's license or a commercial liability insurance policy. *Wagons ho,* I thought.

I waited. Potential drivers continued to be interviewed, and most left issued with blue nylon bags containing all they needed to be independent business drivers. I began to fidget again and casually assessed how bad the injuries could be from a leap from a four-story window. The numbers were dwindling; I was three digits away from the walk of the blue nylon bag. One after another, fortune seekers negotiated with the staff in charge of recruiting drivers. Over and over again, I heard reasons why the background checks were wrong or that a person really did have car insurance but had lost the insurance ID cards. One young man was swearing that he thought his insurance was paid. Briefly, I visualized this guy in front of a judge, swearing he thought the girl was eighteen.

Finally, my number was called, and I nervously approached two white banquet tables arranged side by side. I turned around, looking behind me like a child who had been left at summer camp for the first time. Ms. Taco Bell 2014, taco juice outlining her mouth and a ripe piece of green lettuce lodged on her right canine tooth, smiled at me. She was giving me a supportive thumbs-up sign with both of her chubby mitts. I was wearing a navy blazer, gray pants, and an open-collared blue oxford shirt. Behind the tables were four Uberites. None appeared older than thirty.

My representative was a thin youngster outfitted in three-day beard growth, skinny black jeans, black horned-rim glasses, high-top Converse shoes, and a white T-shirt. I believe the term for this young man would be *hipster*. He looked at me and paused for several seconds, then finally asked, "Can I help you, sir?"

I replied, "Yes, I'm here to activate my driver's application." He paused again, looked at my file, and sat idle for another ten seconds. He asked me if I was aware of how this system worked and if I really wanted to do this. I said, "Yes, I'm here. I did the paperwork." And then, I smiled and nodded. I thought, *You're asking ME if I'm aware of how this works? Look around the room, Einstein.*

He asked, "Why are you doing this?"

"It's cheaper than online dating." He looked stunned, and before he could say anything, I quickly said, "I wanted to earn some extra money"—and smiled and nodded. Methodically, he processed and verified the documents with a great deal of certainty. He handed me a blue nylon bag and told me to familiarize myself with the phone and with the company's protocols. I stood there, and an awkward feeling came over me. *What now?*

The young man looked up at me and said, "Good luck." Slowly I left the room, taking in my last breath of rehabbed loft musk while the arguments about drivers' ratings, insurance coverage, and background checks continued to rage. I slowly wandered out of this strange place, listening to the floorboards creak below my unstable feet.

I drove home on that gray and chilly early spring evening feeling a bit bewildered and not totally certain about proceeding with this lark. When I arrived home I moved the blue bag to the trunk of my car and tried to forget about it. After a few days, every time I approached my car, I glanced sideways at the trunk as if something dark and shameful were lurking in there. I continued to pursue the other endeavors in my life and viewed my car's trunk with an uneasy and unanswered question. The blue nylon bag in the trunk was reminiscent of an adolescent's stash of dirty magazines in the sock drawer.

For a good three weeks I procrastinated, vacillating over the outcomes of experiencing the rideshare world while trying to understand its business practices and their disruptions. Still, I could not bring myself to pull the trigger. My concerns weren't for my physical safety, but for my professional persona and family reputation. Would this kill my professional endeavors? Would I embarrass my sons if they knew? OK, was it safe? Would I pick up people who knew my family and me? Little did I comprehend that I would soon learn how shallow and insignificant those worries were.

The need to resolve the issue of the secret in my trunk weighed heavily on my mind. Finally, I decided to confide in a couple of close friends about this potential project. Both friends realized I would be leading a dual life as a strategic business consultant during the week and a rideshare driver on weekends. One, a professor at a prestigious Chicago business school and a partner in a few of my business ventures, thought it would be fascinating and challenging. He liked the subject matter of the potential research paper and said, "Be careful, and why not?" He proceeded to tell several taxi-driver jokes and then kindly eased up on my battered ego.

The other, a longtime confidant, as well as a good friend, with a background in personal security and paramilitary operations, thought it was a good idea, but he had concerns. The greatest issue on his mind was the fact that I would be driving in the city that leads the nation in gun violence. He thought long and hard and said, "Come to my supply room. I have a few gifts for you." The first thing he handed me was a bulletproof pad for the back portion of my driver's seat.

I asked him candidly, "Joe, do you think this is necessary?"

He replied, "I wouldn't do this without one of these on the seat of my car." He then handed me a disguised tool that would immobilize an aggressive passenger.

"Joe, why do I need this flashlight?" I told him, "No need for a flashlight—I have a good one in the trunk of my car."

He calmly smiled. "Watch this." The innocent flashlight had a special button. When that button was pressed, it gave out a loud crackling noise and blue currents blasted out from around the flashlight lens. I was startled and jumped back five feet, uttering a few choice words. It was a Taser. He looked at me, smiled, and said: "Enjoy this little toy and make it your friend."

The secret in my trunk had grown from a taxi business in a bag to include a bulletproof back pad, and a way to protect myself. I was approaching the point of no return. The next three months would be theater on wheels, playing out on the more than 55,000 miles of Chicago streets and highways with a supporting cast of 2.7 million Chicagoans, as well as a sampling of the 46 million tourists who visit this great city.

The stage was set. What I did not realize was that over the next ninety or so days, each time the curtain opened, every belief I had and every emotion I carried would be taken to their limits. My faith in my fellow man would disappear and that would eventually alter my ability to trust anyone. I would see the normal distribution of humanity and experience the outliers with a new, slightly tainted view of the statistical term *standard deviation*. Emphasis on the deviation, not the standard.

The soundtrack for this extravaganza would be supplied by satellite radio and my iPod stuffed with eclectic music. The car and I were ready to roll. The Mercedes got nick named Hi Ho as in *Hi Ho, Silver* (I know that wasn't your first thought). Hi Ho's suspension and my lower back were soon to feel the rigors of Chicago's potholes, pedaling warriors, and texting pedestrians. Neither Hi Ho's ball joints nor my spine would ever be the same.

DASHBOARD PSYCHOSIS

The month of May passed, and I was a seasoned veteran of the weekend game of Chicago transportation roulette. I had well over one hundred sorties under my belt and I had become smooth and efficient behind the wheel. People close to me were noticing subtle changes in my disposition. Less inclined was I to take attitude from anyone, and I was far more aggressive in my day-to-day actions and thoughts, as if I were fighting for a lane on the road in heavy rush hour traffic. During the week, functioning in his normal world, Pat felt like he had a dark little secret, his alter ego, Patrick. A bizarre aura of funk and cool was gestating under his monogramed shirt and Hermes tie.

The grid of the city was etched in my gray matter, and I now rarely called on the GPS as a crutch. I wanted to drive the riskiest of neighborhoods, explore the areas that were foreign and strange to me. This was what I craved.

My senses grew stronger with each fare, as did my ability to rapidly size up the strange person getting into the car. My heightened abilities to be aware of traffic, pedestrians, cyclists, police, and the carnage in my backseat all at once made me feel like a conductor in front of his orchestra. Steering the direction of conversations with passengers became a favorite pastime. *What's behind all this erratic and uncharacteristic behavior?* I wondered about myself. Was it the constant bombardment of my senses every weekend?

I've described the physical debilitation that a night of driving caused in this old man, but the experience was having the reverse effect on my mind. I was sharper and quicker, and I felt mentally as if I were thirty years younger. Gone were my Oxford shirt and khakis, replaced by a white T-shirt, blue jeans, and sandals. Gone was the timid salutation of "Good evening. Where would you folks like to go?" It had been replaced with, "Hey, where are we off to?" Patrick smoked cigarettes between fares (frowned upon by the company), cleaned the air with Ozium, and said to himself, "If they don't like it, too bad. Screw 'em, it's my ride." I even kept my cigarettes rolled up in the left sleeve of my T-shirt for a more realistic and aggressive look and feel. I was free inventory to the rideshare company anyway. I had found strange new fun in an unsettling and foreign psychological play zone on weekend nights.

Novelty is short lived, and my fun would soon be replaced with anxiety, trauma, and internal conflict. No longer did I need the shelter of Starbucks to transform from Pat to Patrick. The two personalities were on a collision course. I would set my car up for the evening in the driveway of my home for all to see.

I was on the road again, this time giving a Thursday night a spin. Thursday night is the new Friday night I had recently learned. It's when the fine young cannibals whom I drove on Friday and Saturday nights cranked up their alcohol tolerance levels for the upcoming weekend. The emergence of Thursday night as a party night had to be a byproduct of a business concept that I'd always despised: Casual Friday.

This was going to be a real test of my mettle. I was planning on three nights in a row, with a goal of making it to one-thirty a.m. at a minimum every night. As I started that first Thursday, it was five p.m. and the weather was gray and stormy. I didn't know what this extended weekend was going to throw at me, but soon I would find out that there was a significant amount I hadn't yet seen as a rideshare driver.

Landing in the Loop at five-thirty, I saw a herd of people running for commuter trains under umbrellas or the ever-protective newspaper. No cabs were to be had in the rain, and it was pure chaos on the roads. Because of the volume of focused pedestrians, making a turn onto a one-way downtown street could take more than twenty minutes.

Directed by the iPhone, I was off to the Merchandise Mart, where I picked up two women over fifty years of age, a rarity in the world of rideshare passengers. They were pleasant and told me they had two stops. The first lady needed to go to Water Tower Place and the other to West Randolph Street. The total distance of this trip was roughly two and a half miles. On a normal day, this is a twenty-minute trip, but the rain was falling like walls of water and traffic was halted as the sewers of the city backed up, belching water onto the streets and creating areas of deep, standing sewer water on the roads.

The gals in the car were old friends, and they were in Chicago for the National Furniture Show. They were catching up on family and friends, and because of their conversation, they lost all concept of how long they had been in the car. The first lady exited at Water Tower, leaving me with the other woman to have a pleasant conversation about what a beautiful and wonderful city Chicago is. We arrived at the final destination and I wished her well. I switched the iPhone application to *ride completed* and waited for the fare to be tabulated. The next thing I knew, the amount of $78.96 appeared on the phone.

Damn, I thought. *There has to be a mistake.* But there was no mistake. The weather and time of day had created intense demand, forcing the rideshare company to command a higher fare, six times higher, to be exact. The women had been in the car for one hour and twenty minutes. With the fare multiplier, that was the total amount debited from one lady's checking account. I was shocked and thought for sure that they were going to complain, but they never did. I hoped they were in Chicago on a corporate expense account and could get the fee reimbursed. *Damn,* I thought. *They could have rented a room for that amount of money.* In the words of Eddie Rabbitt, "I love a rainy night."

The parade of drenched commuters continued. Driving in the business district at night had a totally different feel than being the designated driver for a large percent of the recent Big Ten graduates who had moved to Chicago. I finally migrated up to Old Town and landed back into my role of shuttling the young and the restless. Bar stops comprised about sixty percent of a normal weekend night's business. I also had brief trips of sweaty women with yoga mats thrown into the mix and people filling my trunk with groceries. I even had a couple with a small dog in a carrier. They were headed to a dog-friendly bar that was hosting a trivia contest. The Chicago bar scene has something for everyone. The night was steady, nothing unique except for the addition of grocery shopping and laundromat excursions, which I surmised must be a part of the weeknight rideshare routine.

The demand was incredible, and the rain was not letting up. I was called to a corner on Chicago Avenue near Elston. Waiting for me was a soaked guy with shoulder-length blond hair, a green poncho, and a sopping wet golden retriever. I pulled up, put the passenger window down, and said to the guy, "You're kidding, right?" I love dogs, but let's put this in its proper perspective. Eighty pounds of wet fur shaking itself to get dry in the backseat of the car was not going to happen. The car would smell and there would be water everywhere. On a dry day, I would have no issue with the dog. The guy looked at me and told me it was because of the dog that he had called for the rideshare. I felt bad, but there was no way. I'm sure he issued a formal complaint.

Then I got summoned to the Gold Coast. To my shock, an extremely elderly woman with a hat and white gloves got into the car. She told me in a scolding manner that she had a list of errands and I was to assist her with her parcels. Who the hell uses the term *parcels* anymore? She had to go to the dry cleaner, the pharmacy, and the grocery store. When we left the dry cleaner, she was upset that her clothes might wrinkle in the trunk. (In this weather, I was not going to hang her cleaning and block my view out a window.) She then got on my case about my dress. She asked if the agency that employed me and allowed me to drive "this nice car" had a dress code. I think she would have liked me to have worn a little black driver's hat and a tie.

Pat was getting a little ticked off, but then he realized that she was near eighty and had discovered disruptive technologies. *Sharp old lady,* I admitted. I was ready to do my best Morgan Freeman impression and tell old Daisy in the backseat that if she didn't knock it off, I wouldn't be driving her to the Piggly Wiggly to get her parcels of groceries. But I restrained myself. Yes, I guessed I was two for two in the complaint department on this rainy night, and my coveted rating of 5.0 was quickly headed to a 4.5 over a dog and a failure to fetch parcels correctly.

The night got older, and the commuters and the mundane chore excursions faded to black. I was running the party crowd now, and the car was rarely devoid of a passenger. I was buzzed to a side street in Lakeview and began the ritual of trying to find the fare on the street. Two guys and a rather large woman got into the car. One of the guys sat in the front passenger seat and the other two sat in the backseat. They gave me an address on Broadway in an area known to Chicago as Boystown.

Over the past several weeks, I had had several gay passengers request locations in that area, and it was no different than any other fare or destination, but this fare *was* different. I sensed it immediately. The fella in the backseat was thin and shaking, with rotten teeth. The fella in front kept telling him he would get his medicine when they got to the bar.

I have a meth addict in my backseat, I thought. The large, menacing-looking woman, I ascertained was their *hag*. She sat there quietly. Having a shaking meth addict in my backseat was bad enough, but the situation soon became even more bizarre.

The thin, lanky guy in the front passenger seat was wearing leather bracelets roughly four inches wide, with two-inch, pointed steel spikes protruding in all directions. He turned, facing the backseat, and talked to his female companion. As he talked, he gesticulated in wild, theatrical motions. With each new brandishing of his arms and hands, the bracelet got nearer to my right cheek. Pat was getting concerned and irritated, but realized there was only one of him and three of them, one a shaking meth addict and another an angry-looking four-hundred-pound princess. My little device in the driver-side door pouch probably wouldn't do me much good against three people, and I realized that anything less than a rhino gun would not stop Meth Boy.

Meanwhile, the great orator's bracelet was getting closer and closer to my face. I realized that he knew what he was doing and that he was playing a mind game with me. I approached a red light and I stopped. Turning to him, Patrick looked him square in the eye and said, "Hey, pal, what do you think of the State of Illinois's new concealed carry law?" (The state of Illinois had just approved the law allowing certified citizens to carry concealed handguns.) Patrick stared him straight in the eye for at least twenty seconds. The light turned green, but he did not move the car. He just froze. The cars behind him were honking their horns and flashing their high beams, but he just stared.

Bracelet Boy said, "I have no opinion, and we're getting out here." They exited Hi Ho pronto. I figured that he figured he had a fifty-fifty chance that I was carrying a gun, and he didn't feel lucky. Patrick drove away listening to the Beatles' "Helter Skelter." Firing up a cigarette, he felt that strange feeling of empowerment, as well as the adrenaline rush, from dodging a potentially dangerous situation by astute thinking on his feet. Then Pat kicked Patrick in the mental ass, because that gamble could have backfired and Bracelet Boy could actually have been the one carrying a gun. I then thought about my banker, my lawyer, my broker, and my other business executive buddies and wondered if they had experienced this crazy type of situation and what they would have done.

I had to decompress a bit after my episode with Hercules and his flesh-piercing bracelets, so I decided to get some coffee, stretch, and, you guessed it, some bladder relief. Hell, I'm over fifty. Sitting there in Boystown traffic, I made a wry observation of myself: I looked like the married suburban guy down here on the down low, stepping out of his traditional marriage, searching for a little boy-on-boy action. As I sat at a red light on Broadway, I looked through my windows at the bears, the twinks, and others and wished I had purchased the tinted glass option for my car. I hoped that no one I worked with would see me and jump to the aforementioned conclusion. Then I said to myself, "Wait a minute. If someone does see me, what the hell are they doing here, anyway?"

After that moment of brilliance, I proceeded to one of my usual doughnut stops. As I walked in, Abdul smiled and said hello. "Mr. Patrick, I have fresh, reduced-fat blueberry muffins for you." I gave him a thumbs up and proceeded to the men's room. By now, I no longer hid the rideshare gear. The cabbies knew who I was and what I did. They mostly said hi and were pretty cool to me, the parasite driver of their industry.

With my coffee and muffin, I went to the car to consume them in peace. Suddenly I realized that on weekends, my world was that dashboard. It was my home, my entertainment, and my life support; during these myopic two-day time frames, Hi Ho had become an extension of Patrick. Had I become Patrick? What had happened to Pat? I did this job only on the weekends, but it consumed my thoughts the entire week. *What is going on here?* I asked myself. My tailbone was throbbing so badly that I had to elevate my torso from the seat and twist from left to right for relief. My right leg was numb and occasionally produced an ankle-to-thigh shooting pain when I pressed the brake pedal. I cringed as my leg began to throb, but I didn't want to stop this incredible adventure. I couldn't stop.

Back on the road, I was heading east on North Avenue, surrounded by taxicabs and an armada of late-model four-door sedans. Unexpectedly, my iPhone turned red; it was bonus fare time in Wicker Park. Suddenly, several of the taxis and many of the four-door sedans pulled sharp U-turns and headed west to Wicker Park, making me realize how many rideshare drivers were on the road. We were like fish racing to the top of the aquarium when the flakes were dropped on the surface of the water. It looked like a synchronized driving event, as if Pavlov had turned a light on or rung a bell, spurring our vehicles to the land of milk and honey.

Being the contrarian that I am, I decided to stay the course, deducing that if all the demand shifted to Wicker Park, it would be only a matter of time before the bell went off and the lab rats rushed back from Wicker Park to Old Town. I was pleased that a few remnants of my graduate school economics course were still working in my brain, as I took note of the shift in supply and the potential underserved demand.

My rhythm came back to me in Old Town. I drove several local bar-to-apartment runs, and all was good. My blood pressure returned to normal, my brush with facial scarring now well behind me. My fares pushed me north, near Lakeview and Lincoln Park, but all was smooth. I sat at a red light at Webster and Elston and thought about a dear business associate who I had done some work for at one of my companies. His tie company was a half block away in a loft that had hosted me and my associates for many a serious strategy session. I wondered what he would think if he called for a ride and then learned I was his driver. Nice people and easy addresses were plentiful and I was sliding into the last few hours of the night feeling good.

Late Thursday had become Friday. At one-thirty in the morning, I got buzzed. I stared at the phone. Do I really want to take this, or should I head home? Oh, what the hell. It would be an easy local shot and I'd be home by two. A couple minutes later I was pulling up to a bar behind Wrigley Field. Two young white guys opened the back door, threw a girl in her early twenties into my back seat, and ran away.

Note to self: It is never good when someone throws a fare into the car and runs away. She was a chunky little cherub. She lifted herself off the floor of the car and chirped happily, "Hello. Who are you?"

I had gambled and I had lost. This already didn't appear to be that last easy money trip I had expected. "Where do you wish to be taken?"

"I don't know my address," she replied and laughed, falling back into the car's rear seat.

"Alright," I said, taking a deep breath. "Can I see your driver's license, so we can read your address and get you home?"

"I only have my debit card," she laughed again in reply. She told me to just drive up and down streets and she would recognize her house. I drove up Addison and my passenger went from a giggly little drunk to a little terror—and a character in one of my future worst nightmares—shouting, "This isn't it!" I turned down Sheffield, and she yelled, "No, you idiot, this isn't it either!" I cautioned myself to keep everything calm because this was getting very uncomfortable. She sat up, and the cherub returned. Leaning forward and rubbing my right shoulder, she said, "You remind me of my daddy."

This isn't good, Pat thought and he kindly told her not to touch him.

The mean girl reappeared. "Are you getting weird with me?"

There I was driving around at two a.m. with some girl young enough to be my daughter and drunk enough to not know where she lived. The leather-studded bracelets were looking good by this time. Pulling over, I pleaded with her to focus and remember her address. She blurted out, "Something to do with a lot of fucking trees." Great. Now I was playing charades with a smashed member of the purple-dinosaur generation in the wee hours.

As if it weren't already bad enough, she was starting to fall asleep, and I wasn't any closer to knowing where this bundle of irresponsibility lived. She nodded off, and I was driving aimlessly through the early morning with one clue. "Something to do with a lot of fucking trees," Patrick muttered. The dark depths of Lincoln Park have a lot of trees, and from a sinister place inside he envisioned her sleeping it off on a park bench. When he regained his less sadistic senses, his mind was still vaulting from one scenario to another.

Out of the clear blue, Pat regurgitated the last stanza of a Robert Frost poem. "And, tired of aimless circling in one place, Steer straight off after something into space."

Where the hell did that come from? Is he losing it? Patrick thought. *I'm losing it.*

I returned to where this pint of tequila with legs had entered my car. The bar was closed and empty. The two charitable dudes who had gift-wrapped and tossed this little daddy-fetish basket of joy into my car and life were long gone. I was rolling sevens at this point.

Pulling back into traffic, I realized that we had originally gone west, so I decided to drive east and wake her up and just maybe something would jog her over-served memory. East we went on Addison. While I was sitting at a light, some force from above focused my eyes on a street sign. Pinegrove. *Something to do with a lot of fucking trees!* This must have been how Columbus's sailors felt when they first saw a bird after months at sea. I pulled over at Pinegrove and Addison and woke her up.

Lifting her drooling head from my car seat, she pointed to the yellow brick apartment building and said, "That one up there." I watched her stumble, but she did it, got into the building and through the lobby. I sat staring at the dashboard and said a prayer of thanks that she was out of my car and life.

At three-fifteen I arrived home, after listening to Crosby, Stills, Nash and Young sing "Teach Your Children Well" the entire way. Then, relief. I could sleep in because I had nothing on my calendar for Friday, except for a twelve-thirty lunch appointment at my club with a private equity firm. I set my alarm for ten-thirty a.m. and fell into a deep, deserved sleep.

At six a.m., my personal cell phone rang. "Are you my Uber driver?"

What the hell? I am nobody's anything at six a.m., especially after last night. "Who the hell is this?"

Well, she was Little Miss Pinegrove and Addison, and she had left her phone in my car and needed it in thirty minutes. Gently I explained to her that that dog didn't hunt, and she would get her phone when I was good and goddamn ready to deliver it. I hung up the phone and sunk back into dreamland.

Twenty minutes later, my phone rang. Guess who? "Do you live at this address?" She gave me my exact address.

Pat yelled, "What the hell are you trying to do to me?" She told me that she had an application that located her phone when it was lost, and she wanted to share with me where it was located. I hung up.

Finally at nine a.m., I answered her fifth call and said, "Give me your address."

I delivered the phone to her, like an obedient rent-a-servant, at her office in River North. So pleasant was she, and with absolutely no residual effects from overconsumption eight hours prior. I asked her what time she started her workday. Hell, we were buddies by now, and I was a lot like dear old Dad, so I felt no hesitation to ask her anything. She replied that she had to be at her desk by seven a.m. Pat whistled under his breath. *Most impressive. This kid is a pro at twenty-three.*

Later in the day, Pat had lunch with a partner from a prestigious private equity firm. He sat across from him and wondered what this guy would think if he knew about the events of his past twelve hours. As the partner spoke, Pat heard nothing. His mind was on the streets, and the only voices he heard were those of his passengers from the night before.

Night fell and there I was again, behind the dashboard of trusty Hi Ho. I was turning right when, to my horror, I didn't see the fixed-gear cyclist. I heard the bending of steel and crushing of bones as an unseen fixed-gear cyclist was swallowed under the front passenger wheel of my car. As the helmeted bike enthusiast slid to the pavement, I could see his fingernails grab the fender and dig into the silver metallic finish of my car. It was like watching a young man being fed to a large garbage disposal. The sleep deprivation had run its wicked course on me.

I was devastated. A crowd of hostile young cyclists began gathering around the car and slamming their fists against the driver's side window. I panicked while I screamed, "Call an ambulance! Call an ambulance!" They grew even more incensed that their two-wheeled comrade was lying motionless under the silver Benz. I woke up.

It was just a nightmare. The T-shirt I slept in was soaking wet with perspiration, and my heart was pounding so profusely that I wondered if the banging in my chest was a nightmare as well. I stood up, looked at the clock, and realized I had been asleep only fifteen minutes. I was shaking as if this tragic event had actually occurred. Sitting on the edge of the bed, I lit a cigarette and realized how many risks we take when challenging the streets of the third most congested city in the country. I thought hard to decipher if the Little Miss Pinegrove Avenue situation was dream or reality. This dual life was beginning to take its toll on me, and I had been living it for only a little over a month.

I knew I had to get back to sleep if I wanted to push iron that night, but the fun and games of being Patrick, the Uber guy, had left me, already superseded by a sobering focus on my new approach to my driving, my passengers, and the ever-stimulating surroundings.

My sleep issues were just beginning. Over the next few months, I would repeatedly wake up from the dream of a bicyclist lodged under the frame of my car. I would grab my pillow, as a person in the backseat tried to lay a blade across my throat. I would wake up screaming, "Check my GPS. It wasn't me!" as I was falsely accused of raping a young female fare. I would wake, suddenly panicked that I was driving in a neighborhood that had no way out, an Escher staircase leading only back to itself. My nocturnal theater throbbed with the faces and voices of the people I had driven just hours before. The dreams became so vivid that at times I could not differentiate between what I had really experienced the night before and what the REM gods dished out for my exhausting driving efforts.

My personality began to change significantly, as did all aspects of my life. I became guarded and suspicious of everybody and everything around me. People close to me noticed a far more aggressive and far less tolerant person. I started to manifest the attitude of an urban survivalist, as I honed a street edge at a late stage in life. Gone was Pat, the gentleman, a member of a fine city club. I *was* Patrick, the guy taking these rich young people to the next grazing hole that was the latest rage for dinner. *I* was the old man driving these brats to their next drink or piece of ass. My mind was distorting daily realities into nightmares, and I was becoming a person of the late-night streetscape. Cabbies, hookers, drug dealers, partiers, cops, and wee-hour loiterers became my new cohorts. I was the mad scientist in a fifties B movie experimenting on myself, and this experiment was playing havoc with my senses and perspective. But I couldn't stop. I had to take this ride further, embracing the dangers and smirking at the risks.

SWEATPANTS, LATIN MUSIC, AND QUALITY PEOPLE

During the previous week, Pat had a busy schedule, but Patrick insinuated himself into Pat's thoughts and actions. Pat was having lunch with an attorney who was boasting about his daughter living in Wrigleyville with some of her sorority sisters. "They're having a ball," he beamed. Patrick emerged in a cartoon bubble above Pat's head wondering if it had been this lawyer's little princess in the backseat of his car last Saturday night while some guy she had just met was digging for gold under the front of her miniskirt.

Pat smiled and nodded as he tried to dispel the visual in his head. "Oh, to be young again," he feigned a jocular chuckle and tried to bring the conversion back to the business at hand. After lunch Pat had a good talking to himself about fantasy and reality...and Patrick's place.

It was the middle of June and summer was in full swing in Chicago. All week, the firm, Uber, had been sending me text messages about the upcoming busy weekend, which would include the Puerto Rican Festival, the Gold Coast Art Fair, and the two-day Spring Awakening

Rock Concert at Soldier Field, as well as the usual summer activities—ballparks, beaches, yadda yadda. I discarded my suit, tie, and wingtips. Donned in white T-shirt, blue jeans, and sandals, it was time for Patrick to hit the road. I made sure my trusty defense toy was fully charged and that it could deliver adequate voltage to keep me safe. I cranked up Billy Joel's "Travelin' Prayer" and put the pedal to the metal. Driving south on Western Avenue, I immediately noticed several cars displaying Puerto Rican flags, with proud passengers playing loud Latin music and wearing well-lit smiles.

"Hell," I smirked to myself and nodded in approval. "It's only six p.m. This is gonna be a fun and crazy weekend."

The night was fast and the local rides plentiful. The weather was perfect, and before I knew it, it was ten-thirty p.m. and I had earned $150. The goal was to make it to the witching hour of three a.m.

A buzz came from Old Town, and I picked up two couples in their mid to late twenties. They had just had dinner together and were making plans for future social events. The first pair left the car and I was left with a cuddly duo in the backseat. This guy had a Southern accent and, from what I could ascertain, he was a member of some three-letter government law enforcement agency—or that was what he wanted everyone in the car to believe. The woman was attractive and wearing the usual black yoga pants and sheer white top.

He remarked of the couple who had just exited, "They're a quality couple, and they're the type of people you should socialize with, not your slutty friends."

Ouch, Pat thought.

She replied, "But baby, I only went to clubs with the girls last year when we weren't seeing each other."

The guy sounded condescendingly authoritative. "Well, that was then, and now I will introduce you to quality people."

I urgently wanted to tell this guy where to go, but I just turned and sarcastically smiled and nodded. Then things got interesting. She asked him if he was going to stay the night at her place. He firmly responded no and that he wanted her to stay at his place. She insisted. He continued to talk to her like she was a child. She told him she had to stay at her place because of her dog.

He replied, "We can go walk the dog and then go to my place." She told him that she couldn't leave the dog home alone because it would bark all night and the neighbors would get upset. He replied, "That's too bad."

By now she was pleading with him that she wanted to cuddle and wake up next to him. *Come on, Adonis. Give the chick a break,* I thought.

Then she said, and I quote, "I'll do that special thing you like if you stay."

I told myself for the first of many times, *I couldn't create this shit if I were writing fiction.*

He said (more quoting here), "You'll do that special thing anyway."

The girl was bummed when we arrived at her place. She climbed out, and Mr. Wonderful said to me, "Driver, wait here ten minutes."

Oh yes, sir, Sergeant Asshole, sir, Patrick thought. *What an arrogant jerk,* Pat scowled to himself, as he pondered "that special thing." This guy is getting his dome buffed in the vestibule, as the "driver" waits for his triumphant return. Patrick ruminated on the "quality" of the characters participating in this blessed event.

Captain America got back to the car six minutes later. *Six minutes,* I thought to myself. *What a stud.* By the time you take into account unzipping, zipping, and shirt tucking, either she was a vacuum cleaner or he was a quick-shot artist. I hope his motto wasn't to serve and protect. I drove him to his place while listening to the Rolling Stones' "Sad Sad Sad," then continued to roll into the city's night.

The concert at Soldier Field ended at eleven-thirty p.m. This was a really young crowd, a demographic who liked to pack five or more sweaty, loud people into a car. Now that's sharing economy. Quickly my advanced driver's senses told me to avoid that part of the city. I was summoned to the Gold Coast, and off I went, still thinking about the earlier couple and the "quality people" the young lady was going to be introduced to by Sir Lancelot. *Will the rest of these quality people like a quickie in the vestibule too*, I often wondered.

After I had waited for fifteen minutes, a tall, thick, attractive blonde, about thirty, emerged from the posh high-rise building. *She's a tall girl,* Patrick thought, and mused to himself, *Hell, I would work with a net under me if I fell off giving that ride a turn.* She was carrying a cardboard box in one hand. With her other hand, she was clutching a pair of oversized men's gray sweatpants that were a good twelve inches too large for her at the waist. A burgundy evening bag hung from her right shoulder. As she entered the car, I turned and helped with the box. I couldn't help but notice a burgundy bridesmaid's dress, corsage, and a large pair of burgundy pumps in the box. She gave me an address near Wrigley Field. She didn't say a word, but as I drove, I noticed a certain smell.

It is common knowledge that when two people have relations, it can get a bit gamey. This sweetheart had to have had her salad tossed every which way a few times because the subclimate in my car was getting ripe and downright nasty. I opened my window halfway for relief. This was something of a post-reception ride of shame. I considered how big the sweatpants were and the oversized boat shoes I noticed on her feet and realized that my good-looking Amazonian had just tussled with a wooly mammoth.

We arrived at her apartment near Wrigley Field. It was a respectable joint, but a far cry from North Dearborn Parkway where I had picked her up. She noticed there was a homeless man sitting in the well-illuminated doorway of her apartment building and asked if I would wait until she was in the lobby before I left. I said absolutely. I always waited until my female passengers entered their residences before I pulled away. Call Pat old-fashioned, but he felt more comfortable knowing that they were securely in their buildings before he left.

She was at the door, holding the box under her right arm, clutching the waist of the oversized sweats with her left hand, and trying to extract her keys out of the small evening bag. The next thing I knew, she inadvertently released the pants and they fell to her ankles. Her nice, round, shapely rear was bent over and well-lit for all to see. The homeless guy looked up with a creepy smile on his face. She was fumbling to get the evening bag and dropped the box and now had to turn around, displaying the front portion of her lower torso. My immediate thought was that there must be a lot of money in the waxing business. I waited while she quickly gathered her belongings so her half-naked body could hustle through the finally-unlocked door. I drove away telling myself yet again, *Nobody's going to believe this shit when I write the book*. The iPod played "You Sexy Thing" by Hot Chocolate.

What a night! I cocked my head and gave a low whistle as a mint-condition, yellow 1964 Chevy Biscayne low-rider blew by Hi Ho with a six-foot-wide Puerto Rican flag waving out of the back window. Our Lady of Guadalupe seemed to be affixed to the rear window of every other car sharing the road that night. The streets were jumping, with people everywhere: four-door sedans waiting with flashing lights for fares, cabbies aggressively snagging rides, and drunken people stumbling into the streets, while others crossed at will with no regard for oncoming traffic. That type of behavior would trigger one of my many newly conditioned sardonic retorts: "Three thousand pounds multiplied by thirty miles an hour. Do the math, asshole. I think you're going to lose."

The potholes created by the brutal winter were still rife with rim-cracking edges, even into mid-June. The driving was aggressive. Not only had my personality changed, but so had my driving habits. Patrick was now fierce, and began to view commandeering Hi Ho as an element of his work performance and an extension of his new, edgy street persona. He floated through traffic, changing lanes with precision and cunning. In addition, he had perfected one of the quickest and most demonstrative one-finger salutes ever seen. He was feeling it. He even once referred to ever-trustworthy Hi Ho as "this taxi cab" to a passenger. Hi Ho was so upset that the check engine light instantly blinked on.

The night pulsed on, and I had over $280 in the bank. At two a.m., a buzz came from Wicker Park. Pulling up to the front of a bar, I saw my fare waiting, a woman in her mid-thirties. She approached the car, held the door open, and said to a slightly overweight version of Fabio with shoulder-length brown hair and shirt unbuttoned to the navel, "Are you getting in?" They looked at one another with disgust and anger. What's with guys and shirts unbuttoned to the navel? Is that code for "I'm an asshole"?

This indecision and tension went on for about seven minutes, and then he finally got in the car with a nasty scowl on his face. Once in the backseat, he grabbed the rear passenger door handle with both hands, slamming the door as hard as I had ever heard a car door slam. I turned around and stared at him. He looked at me and said, "What the fuck are you looking at?"

I replied, "Excuse me. This car is not owned by Uber or the Chicago Transit Authority." Patrick stared him in the eyes, and if the eyes are the windows to the soul, Patrick was deep in soulful R&B. "It is my vehicle, so please get your sorry ass out of my car."

He told me, "Shut the fuck up and drive."

I had my little high-voltage friend Sparky cocked and ready to go to work. I'm not a very big person, but I won't back down. Plus, I would have loved to shoot 4000 volts into this guy's obnoxious chest hairs. I gently said, "Get the fuck out of my car now, both of you."

He replied, "I'm going to kick the shit out of you." He worked up a fist, ready to deliver a punch.

Patrick held the Taser in the foot well of the front passenger seat and snapped off a few crackles, smiled, and told them again to get out. The pleasant sound of the Taser made the guy grab the handle and jump out of the car while he told Patrick, "I have your plate number. I'm calling the police."

Patrick snapped off a few more crackles and continued to stare at him with a bit of crazy in his eyes. The woman left with him. I have to admit I was concerned about her safety.

They received the lowest rating possible and I drove away listening to Electric Light Orchestra's "Hold on Tight."

Little did I know that this phenomenon of a couple fighting and bringing the situation into the car would repeat itself with a great deal of regularity. The male of the couple would always displace his aggression for the woman onto the driver. If my taking the abuse prevented one woman from being battered, it was well worth it, but I doubt that was the case. Most of these guys were gutless pigs. I hope they read this.

After making my painful journal entries upon getting home that night, I poured myself two fingers of scotch and had a smoke on the balcony. I was incredibly wound up and probably not just from staring at a clenched fist. My focus remained on the events of the evening, and I started to feel two forces within me challenge each other as I zoned out. Force number one was Patrick, who wanted to knock the guy's Chiclets out of his mouth, and force number two was Pat, who was getting concerned about future possible altercations. Pat and Patrick were truly starting to develop into two significantly opposite beings. The moon reflected off the river, and Pat was relieved that he didn't have to deal with any of this shit for a week—or that's what he thought.

The next day, I awaited a visit from the Chicago police, but it never happened. What did happen was the growth of my nasty, streetwise personality, which I am ashamed to admit. My mood grew intensely impatient, and I didn't believe a word anyone said. I started feeling like a mercenary driver. My view of humanity was deteriorating swiftly, and I was developing a permanent scowl. In one night, my eyes had gone from the glow of a sexy blonde's lower torso to the clenched fist of an ignorant, drunken bully. My emotions darted from the titillation of cute sexual exploits to the darkest fear of physical confrontation with a despicable idiot. *Drive on, Patrick,* I thought.

REDEMPTION

Pat's normal weekday routine was becoming a strange, contorted, and silent struggle. His perspective was askew and he judged every other word said to him to be pure bullshit. One day he was in a cab with a client when the client asked him if he knew anything about Uber. In a deadpan voice Pat responded, "I'm researching the industry and when my research is concluded I'll fill you in."

Patrick silently interjected, *Download the app and take it for a spin, you lazy putz*. Normally, Pat would enter a note into his phone after such an observation: *Phil Smith is interested in disruptive industries, get information to him as soon as it is available*. Not this time. He just sat in the cab and felt the uneasy feuding between Pat and Patrick. The same client invited Pat to his country club for dinner in two weeks on a Saturday night. Normally, Pat would graciously accept the invitation. Not this time. Patrick chimed in, silently, eyebrows arched, *And give up the chance to drive your spoiled-ass kids around with white rings around their nostrils and running noses? No fucking way. You're all a bunch of boring blowhards anyway.*

Pat, so quick on his feet, proffered a reason that he couldn't attend, but took a rain check. The fissure that was splitting Pat and Patrick in his psyche was really starting to bother Pat. Or maybe not. Not this time. As he walked away from the cab he rolled his eyes. *Patrick's right. What a boring bourgeois crowd I run with.*

Uber nights were becoming almost routine, except for the occasional new route and a few extraordinary people. It was a late Saturday night in June, and I was now approaching this experiment with a robotic, instinctual methodology. Some fares were self-absorbed, get-me-to-the-next-hedonistic-experience morons. This was not a good emotional place for me.

I knew that at least once every weekend, some stooge would try to pound my brains in and some over-served and overfed party animal would come close to throwing up and destroying the interior of my car. Each weekend, I would hit a pothole so deep I would cringe at what was happening below my fenders. I knew I would get cut off by an aggressive driver, I would have several pedestrians run in front of the car, and I would dodge several dozen cyclists. I also knew I would drive by countless waxing parlors, dog grooming facilities, nail boutiques, and dry cleaners. The frequency of these types of businesses triggered a new business concept: Combine two of these operations into one. Get Fido groomed and kitty waxed at the same location! With free Wi-Fi! That was my new view of what the weekend would hold. Gone were the thrill and coolness of this once novel, exciting, and spontaneous experience. My personality was becoming extremely hardened and I didn't give a damn who knew it.

The faces started to look the same, the outfits were predictable, and the final destinations no longer needed to be looked up on the GPS. I was efficient and almost cocky about my approach to rideshare driving. I even knew where most of the bad potholes were and what streets were good for a fare. The car reeked of a combination of perspiration from those leaving sweaty bars and strange perfumes, similar to a fragrance counter in a department store. My tailbone had a permanent dull pain, and my right leg was always numb. I planned my coffee breaks and went about my weekend excursion like an assembly-line worker with no union representation. I was aggressive, yet at times strangely detached from what I was actually doing with my weekend nights.

Shortly after midnight, a call came from a downtown hotel, and off I went. The fare's name was Terrence. He had a 4.8 rating, and as usual, that was all I knew about my future rider. I waited in front of the hotel, assuming I was waiting for the typical guy or couple having a smashing time on Saturday night, but they never appeared. Instead, a young African-American man tapped on the passenger window. This was exceptional. Typically, people hop in the backseat and give me an address, but not this time. Hitting the window switch, I noticed this young man was wearing restaurant kitchen clothes, not party attire. Expecting someone dressed for being out on the town, I was thrown for a loop.

He leaned into the window and said, "Sir, you can't take me home in this car. My neighborhood is too bad."

Pat looked at him and said, "No, I entered into an implied contract when I accepted this fare. Get in."

He replied, "But, sir—"

Before he could finish, Pat demanded, "Get in."

Reluctantly, he entered the car. This was the first real hot and muggy night of the season, and it appeared that all of Chicago was out enjoying the near-tropical temperatures. He gave me an address off of Madison Street, about two miles west of the United Center. West Side. This is one of the worst neighborhoods in the city for crime, an area riddled with poverty, gang violence, and vice, where a great number of highly publicized shootings and murders occur.

As we pulled away, Terrence began again to lobby that I reconsider this decision, but I would hear none of it. We were off to the West Side well after midnight.

Terrence shared with me how tired he was from a twelve-hour shift of preparing vegetables in one the city's busiest banquet hotels. I shared with him that I was a veteran of restaurant work. He paused and asked if he could ask me a personal question and I replied, "Fire away. Ask what you want."

"What's with the nice car, and where's the ring on your right hand from?" he asked. I came clean and told him I wasn't doing this for the usual reasons people drive Uber, that I was researching a book, and that the ring was from the school where I had received my MBA. He smiled and told me he was putting himself through school at one of Chicago's many fine colleges and he was majoring in marketing. He peppered me with business questions and probed for career advice. We were stuck in traffic, but he didn't care because we were talking business.

His youthful passion was great to see, especially compared to the entitled and stale view of business I often experienced during the day. Stimulated by his interest and curiosity, I felt a little of my old self start to return. He asked many deep, business-focused questions, and I fired answers back and then asked for his opinion on various business subjects, from disruptive industries to the recent boom in the oil fracking industry. I noticed he was enjoying this as much as I was. We weren't a fifty-plus white guy and a twenty-something black man having an insignificant discussion, but two people passionate about business, sharing their thoughts and ideas.

As we exchanged business philosophies, we passed the recently silenced United Center, still mourning the early exit of the Chicago Blackhawks from the playoffs. I didn't know that in a few short minutes, this great experience and conversation were going to take a life-altering change in direction.

About a mile-and-a-half west of the United Center, we hit a scene I could never have imagined. Chicago Police Department squad cars and paddy wagons were on full alert, flashing piercing blue lights on every corner. In addition, people twenty deep were at the corner of the intersection as if it were noon on north Michigan Avenue. This was bad and frightening. Terrence then said with tears in his eyes, "Look at what my neighbors are doing to each other." I had never been speechless with a fare before, but I was in awe of all that was around me. He then said in a quivering voice, "You know, sir, at times some Republicans are correct." (My rule is to not talk about religion or politics with a fare. It is not a good practice to discuss such passionate subjects in the confined quarters of an automobile with a stranger.)

I was dumbfounded and cautiously asked, "Correct about what, Terrence?" in a soft, curious tone.

As I continued to absorb the carnage unfolding just twenty feet away from my car window, Terrence responded, "As long as there are entitlement programs, too many of my people will be kept at this level of poverty and continue to do this to themselves."

With my mouth open in disbelief, I responded instinctively, "Yes, but society does need a safety net for those who cannot help themselves." He perceived that I was freaked out.

As we approached a red light, to my left were an ambulance and four squad cars. I looked at the pavement and saw a heavyset black man lying there, bleeding out of his skull. He was apparently a victim of a gunshot wound. I looked intently and realized that such a thing was unimaginable to the rest of the city. Just a few miles away from this sad horror are the Gold Coast, Hyde Park, and the financial district, yet most of the inhabitants of this city see only small bits of this carnage on the nightly news. Seeing it unfold in front of my eyes delivered an impact like nothing I had ever experienced. The car stayed quiet until Terrence told me to take a right at the next side street. We drove two blocks and arrived at his apartment. I turned, and we shook hands. He asked me, "How are you getting home, sir?"

I replied, "Fast, Terrence, very fast," in a timid and shaken voice.

Here I was at one o'clock in the morning, alone in one of the most terrifying neighborhoods in the country. The only way back downtown was the way I had come, but I did not have the distraction of Terrence and our great conversation, which now seemed like it had taken place a week before instead of only twenty minutes earlier. Turning left on Madison Street, I proceeded east. The blue lights were still flashing, and the crowds of people on the corners were just as big. The people in the crowd were mostly young adults, but I could see a young boy roughly ten years old dancing around the crowd, wearing a Chicago Bulls T-shirt and a pair of well-worn Air Jordan basketball shoes. He tried to get as close to the street as possible, as if he were trying to see what flavor choices the ice cream truck was offering. There were no bells on this ice cream truck, however, just the piercing shrill of an ambulance's siren. How sad.

Six police officers were standing amongst the crowd, sweating through their necessary, but cumbersome, bulletproof vests. One was talking to a man in the crowd while the other five formed a well-choreographed circle around the interviewing officer. The five officers in the circle were moving their heads as if they were on swivels as they surveyed the area. I could see their rapid eye movements absorbing every movement happening around them in the crowd of onlookers. I pulled up and watched as the first responders nervously started the process of transferring the man who was bleeding on the pavement onto a gurney. A large black vinyl bag with a zipper lay next to him.

His open eyes stared motionless into the early summer's night sky. I wondered if he was a father. Was his mother alive? Who was this person whom I had just watched spend the last few moments of his life lying on his back on West Madison Avenue? The obnoxious sound of the ambulance siren and the near-seizure-inducing lights of the squad cars bypassed my external senses and found a resting place deep inside my soul. As I stared at the still body, I realized that this very event was as much a part of what I attempted to experience as the cute girls in the miniskirts en route to bars on Lincoln Avenue. I was overcome with emotion, and all my senses were on overload, absorbing what was happening around me like a day-old sweet roll in hot coffee. Streetwalkers, drug dealers, and neighborhood folk who were part of this tragic cast fascinated me. Witnessing this tragedy play out was wretched and yet somehow exhilarating. No longer was I scared to be there. In a bizarre way, I was glad to be there.

Then I snapped to, aware of what a conspicuous observer I was and drove east, running every red light. I looked to the twin red beacons of the Willis Tower as a young boy does to his mother's waiting arms while the neighborhood bully chases him home from school. Witnessing this was as important to my experience of being a rideshare driver as was the prostitute on Belmont and Sheffield lifting her miniskirt and exposing male parts while I waited for the light to turn green in the middle of the night. This is a nocturnal world that very few people from my socioeconomic demographic experience. No longer was I appalled by any of what I was exposing myself to. I was enthralled. This was not a made-for-television drama. These people were flesh and blood, not 2-D caricatures, not Hollywood creations. It made me understand why Sinclair had needed to see the rats in the packinghouses and

Hemingway had needed to witness the horrors of war firsthand. I then realized that to experience life, I would have to expose myself to all of life, even the ugly, heartbreaking, and catastrophic.

Finally, I stopped at a red light in front of the United Center. I looked to my right, and saw the statues of my boyhood heroes, Bobby Hull and Stan Makita. Staring at the lifeless statues, I knew that their fantastic careers, great as they may have been, paled by comparison to the new heroes I saw this evening: Terrence, and the brave men and women of the Chicago Police and Fire Departments. The radio was playing Harry Chapin's "Taxi" as the ambulance carrying the intimate stranger I had watched leave this planet passed me on the way to a hospital or morgue. Chapin continued to sing about lost love and addiction in a somber ballad as shock and dismay installed themselves in a permanent corner of my soul.

I decided that was enough for one night and shut the iPhone off. I turned off the radio and drove in silence while I pondered all of what had happened in the previous hour. I didn't even realize that I had left the turn signal on; its rhythmic tapping was a metronome setting the pace for my unsettled heartbeat. My mind tried to dismiss the shock and disbelief of what I had just witnessed and my thoughts returned to Terrence. I walked through the entire sequence of events, from his tapping on Hi Ho's window to my dropping him off at his apartment. This young man, after a long day of working on his feet, was more concerned about the health and welfare of a stranger than about himself. During the entire journey, Terrence had referred to me as "sir." He had treated me with the utmost respect. He was driven to change his circumstances through hard work and inquisitive study. He was receptive to views from political figures that would normally run against his assumed beliefs. He had a profound sense of caring for people. He was gentle and wise beyond his years in every sense of the word. I realized that in a night in which I had most likely watched a man die on the street, I had also met a man who made this entire saga of Patrick, the rideshare guy, worth its while. Thank you, Terrence.

CHEAPER THAN ONLINE DATING

The summer weather in Chicago had been gorgeous, and weather of this sort unleashed all the pretty people on the weekends. The front suspension on Hi Ho was feeling very loose, and so were the inhabitants in the car. I felt like a true veteran and I had learned how to be a bit player in this weekly hormonal extravaganza. The fares sensed my confidence, and I was repeatedly asked, "Hey dude, what's with the whip, and why are you doing this?" My standard answer was that it was cheaper than online dating. That usually triggered a laugh and they would ask again, "Really, dude, what's up?"

What most of my young fares were asking was, "What's an old man like you doing this for—and in such a nice car?" The pat online dating response worked for a while, but then I found the magic response: look into the rearview mirror and tell them that I'm writing a book about this very experience. Most of the passengers would get excited and ask how they could be in the book. That question usually disqualified them. They would then ask what a few of the wildest things were that I had seen in my many journeys. I soon found out that sharing episodes of other people losing their inhibitions in my car triggered others to do the same.

Who knows why, but certain types of riders came in bunches. If I picked up a couple that included a crazed and angry boyfriend, chances are I would get three similar couples that night. The same could be said for fares that needed to vomit or who were rude. One particular night seemed to be ladies' night, and I choose that term loosely—no pun intended. It seemed like every fare was a woman or combination of women. A group of four girls in their mid-twenties came into the car. One of them had never experienced a rideshare trip before. Her three partying comrades jumped into the car, but she remained outside and said with terror on her face, "I don't want to get raped." This made me feel just great.

The other three girls were getting comfortable and chatting about the cool car they were riding in. They heckled her and said, "Get your ass in the car, you baby." Poor thing. Because she was the last to enter, she got the privilege of sitting in the front seat.

We headed off to their desired watering hole, and after a few minutes, the girl in front began to relax a little. She told me about all the articles she had read about rideshare drivers taking advantage of their customers. She then told me that all the background check information was false, and that false information was the foundation for her fear. At that point the bizarre nature of strangers buying rides from other strangers hit me again. *How would I feel if I had a daughter and she was in a strange city being shuttled around by a strange old man?* I thought.

Then she started joking and getting into the spirit of the evening. As she was getting out of the car later, she turned to me, gave me a peck on the cheek, and said, "Thank you for not raping us." I sat in the car for a few minutes and tried to process what had just happened in a ten-minute trip.

The night rolled on, and the ladies kept buzzing the phone. I picked up two extremely well-dressed women in their late twenties to early thirties in Wicker Park. What struck me at first was how elegantly and similarly they were dressed. These two were Hepburn-esque in every action and article of clothing and jewelry. They were by far the most classy and sophisticated passengers I had picked up since my research began. They both wore knee-length black dresses with slits up the sides. These dresses were not the skin-tight sausage casings I'd become used to. The fabric flowed gracefully as they walked. Their scent was appropriately dispensed. How nice that someone wasn't bathed in cheap perfume for a change.

This pair entered the car and were quite pleasant. They asked me to take them to Second City, the landmark improvisational comedy club about twenty minutes away. When they first sat in the car, they were each on a separate side of the rear seat. As the car traversed down North Avenue in an easterly direction, I consulted the rearview mirror when changing lanes or avoiding potholes. Every time I looked in the mirror, the two of them were five inches closer to each other. When we were five minutes away from Second City, these extremely pretty ladies could not hold in their lust anymore. They were passionately kissing. One exclaimed, "I have missed you so much," and the other said, "I thought your plane would never land."

Pat looked at himself in the mirror and reminded himself, *Not a word,* and *raise that mirror. Keep your eyes on the road.* Patrick was pissed off at Pat's discretion. We arrived at the club, and they gathered themselves, refreshed their lipstick, and thanked me for the ride. I drove away wondering if anybody with whom I interacted Monday through Friday would ever fathom what a weekend night was like for me.

This night was beginning to be quite interesting. A buzz came from a six-flat apartment building in Lakeview. Four young ladies in evening gowns got in the car. It was rather late to be going to a wedding. "Where are we off to?" I asked. They gave me the address of an apartment building in Lincoln Park. Easy fare. They shared with me that they were not happy to be going to a party that was an attempt to recreate everyone's high school prom. That explained the dresses. *What a devious party theme*, Patrick thought and smiled.

I was listening to the Eagles sing "Take It Easy" at a low volume. Before I knew what was going on, the girl in the front passenger seat turned up the volume and started to sing the lead. The three girls in the back got close and handled the harmonies. It was obvious that they had done this before with this song. To my surprise, the conductor up front pointed to me and commanded, "Let's go, Pops. Join in." We both belted out "Winslow, Arizona" with a laugh and a roar. The backseat was harmonizing, and the car was swaying back and forth. I found it ironic that they were enthusing over a song that was popular thirty years before they were born, when *I* was in high school going to prom. It was fun. Here we were, strangers driving through the city, enjoying the Eagles as if we had all gone to school together.

We pulled up to the address. They didn't want to leave, but they had a commitment. As the last girl was leaving the car, she told me that the inside of the rear passenger door was adorned with snot. *How nice*, I thought, *I have green caulk around my door handle*. Earlier in the night, I must've had a young Warhol finger-painting in my car, his medium: nasal mucous. Ah, all the arts were represented in my car that night, not just the performing arts.

Often as I was left with an empty car after enjoying the spontaneity of fun young people, I would wonder where they all came from. What were their goals and dreams? How much money did these kids spend on a weekend night of drinking and partying? Were they the entitled techno brats my generation thinks they are? Yes, my generation had the Vietnam War and Richard Nixon, but we also had hope and affordable educations as well as jobs available to us when we were ready to work. These kids were inheriting, at an average, $60,000 of the national debt each. Most young people are not recipients of trust funds, and many have tens of thousands of dollars in student loan debt. After amassing the debt, they enter a world that has no place for them. They understandably don't trust anyone on any side of our government. If I were facing their future, I would get high and drunk every weekend night, too. I'm glad some of them were able to sing with an old man who came from a generation who did not trust anyone over thirty.

The shock of going from a festive, lively group in my car to total silence in an area of the city that was foreign to me would usually shock my imagination. As my mind traveled in the quiet car, I'd look at century-old apartment buildings and speculate about what they had witnessed over the years. Did the dreaded Western Union telegram get delivered to that address in the forties? Did a family huddle around a television and watch John-John salute his father's casket in the living room in 1963? Was a heart broken in 1969 when the Mets overtook the Cubs? I'd look at these beautiful structures and realize with envy and astonishment all they had experienced through their residents. These buildings will see history continue to unfold for decades after I become dust. Wisdom learned from the driver's seat of a car. The silence of a car and a happenstance destination can take the imagination on a journey all its own. Pat was reconciling himself with his mortality after a group of young ladies had told him to take it easy.

The phone buzzed, and again, the fare was a woman. The address was the Drake Hotel. As Chicagoans know, the Drake is quite a nice hotel located off of north Michigan Avenue. It's where royalty historically stays when in town. I hustled to get there. I pulled up and waited, watching mostly middle-aged couples exit the hotel in festive, upscale attire. I lost myself staring into space and then was brought back to reality with a tap on the rear window. I hit the unlock button, and three nicely dressed young ladies entered the backseat of the car. The front passenger door opened. A fourth passenger had entered. He smiled. A young man with a face as American as apple pie, he wore a light blue polyester suit, white shirt, black tie, and black patent leather shoes. He extended his right hand and we shook. He introduced himself and let me know that he was from Iowa. Smiling back, I said, "Really? I would have never guessed."

He was a little buzzed but very friendly. I couldn't help but like this kid right off the bat. The Eagles were still softly playing on my iPod, which he was quick to notice. He asked me if I knew where Butch McGuire's was located. I smiled and said, "Sure do. Three blocks away."

It was a quick trip, but he turned around to his three female friends and shouted, "Damn, we're going to the bar in Chicago in a Mercedes Benz." I smiled and found out they were in town for a wedding. We were sitting at a light a half a block away from the bar when he said, "Sir, can I ask a huge favor? When we get dropped off at the bar, can you have the Eagles 'Life in the Fast Lane' blasting?"

I handed him the iPod, saying, "Sure, sport, go crazy." On a warm Saturday night, the patrons of the drinking establishments on Division Street wait in line outside the bars and spill into the streets. My passenger queued the song, and as we arrived at the jammed bar, he opened the car door with the music blasting. The gals got out of the backseat, but then he did something that I have to admit still cracks me up.

The music was playing loudly as he got out of the car, and he left the door open, putting one hand on the top of the car door and the other on his hip, his head slowly surveying the terrain from left to right and then slowly back from right to left. This took roughly two minutes. He turned to me and said, "Now this is what I'm talking about." He reminded me of General Douglas MacArthur, surveying the beach where he had just landed. He slapped me a high five and went on to conquer new territory for the people of Iowa. I loved this guy. He was a three-block passenger who made my night. The fare was $4.35, but worth every fast-lane minute.

No sooner had I dropped off the general than a buzz came from a restaurant near LaSalle and Ontario Streets. The fare was under a female name. Little did I know that this was going to be one of the most unbelievable and erotically shocking rides of this entire experience. Two hours earlier, I'd had two lovely ladies burying their tongues down each other's throats. A few weeks before, I'd had the girl begging a guy to spend the night by promising, "I'll do that special thing you like." Earlier in the month, I'd had to fend off a jerk telling me to comment on his date's ass. What could be worse? This is becoming like something out of a pulpy cheap novel. I mused over the past few weeks, not knowing the best was yet to come. Again, no pun intended.

Two very attractive, young brunette women came into my car carrying small, colorful foil shopping bags with colored tissue paper poking out the top. They were wearing very short skirts, sporting great figures. They gave me a warm, "Hello, Patrick. Great car" and an address about forty minutes north on Lake Shore Drive. As I proceeded to the drive, they asked how my night was going, how long I had been driving, and the usual icebreakers for ride conversation. I noticed the bags and asked if they had been at a wedding. They replied, "No, a bachelorette party." They confessed that while there had been no male stripper at the event, they had been able to purchase sex toys.

"Nice," I said, smiling and glancing in the rearview mirror.

The next thing I knew, I heard the rustling of tissue and one of the young ladies in the rear passenger seat asked me, "Do you want to see what I bought?"

I didn't know what to say, but since it was taking us forever to get to Lake Shore Drive, I said, "Sure, why not?" That triggered the other one to start digging through her goody bag as well.

While we were sitting at a red light, the girl in the right rear passenger seat leaned forward and said, "Look at what I bought." She extended her arm, putting a kelly green, fuzzy-textured object that reminded me of a pizza dough hook attachment for a KitchenAid mixer in front of my eyes. She hit the on switch, and the thing began to buzz and rotate. The next thing I knew, the other young woman was switching on a red phallic device. It was a buzzing duet, another interpretation of *Buzz Ride*. I was laughing and blushing. My young friend with the red device was having second thoughts about not having purchased the green kitchen helper. *Wow, what a story*, I thought.

We finally merged onto Lake Shore Drive, and I assumed the entertainment was over. We were talking about music, the weather— all the normal, superficial banter that gets exchanged in a taxi discussion. Suddenly, I spied a freshly pedicured foot resting on the passenger seat next to me against the headrest. Slowly, another foot emerged on the other side of the headrest and I started to hear a buzzing sound. Next, I felt two feet pressing against the back of my seat and heard a second buzzing. I adjusted the rearview mirror and—you guessed it (you did, right?)—skirts were pulled up, sans knickers, and as usual, hardwood floors appeared. These girls were enjoying themselves. Neither was touching the other. They had just decided it was a good time to try out their new friends. I knew I had to focus on the road, but let's be honest here—it wasn't easy. Patrick was enjoying the hell out of this as Pat kind of tried to remind him that they were commandeering an automobile. I didn't know what to say to my passengers, but Patrick did. "What type of music would you like—maybe some Barry White?" For the record, the young lady with the dough hook seemed to be having more fun. If I can help any female readers with firsthand market research, I say go with the fuzzy kitchen utensil.

They completed their pleasuring activities about five minutes before arriving at their location. They sat up with no shame or embarrassment, put their new buddies away, and lowered their skirts. Their beet-red faces were smiling and they were content with their ride. When I reached their building, they left, saying, "Night, Patrick. You're the coolest."

Alone I sat in the car for a few minutes, having a smoke, making sure that this was not a dream from which I would soon wake, wearing a drenched T-shirt. It was no dream, and I laughed my ass off for a good five minutes, realizing I would never be able to look at my KitchenAid the same way again. I continued to laugh hysterically, saying yet again, "This cannot be happening, and I know that no one will believe this shit." I also didn't realize that in the second phase of this rideshare experiment, when riders found out I was researching a book and asked about the wildest thing to happen in the car, that this story would quickly remove rider inhibitions and lead to similar bizarre behavior.

The footnote to this story is that a few weeks later, I came clean with my twenty-one-year-old twin sons about my Uber life. I shared this event with the boys, and they both had interesting responses. One asked if "all the lady bits were cleaned from the backseat of the car," and the other said in a pained voice, "Dad, you drive us to Sunday brunch in that car." If Hi Ho's backseat could talk, it would sound like a cable television adult special. This had truly been a buzz ride.

The night settled into the normal pattern of returning people home from various bars. I pulled up to one bar and saw two bouncers trying to pick up a young blond girl in a short black dress from the curb, where she was covered in vomit. I drove away. "Not in my ride, doll." I pulled down a side street and saw a Chevy Suburban with livery license plates pulled over. The driver was a tall, heavyset guy in a tuxedo who was standing next to two young ladies in short black dresses (what else?) with their shoes off, leaning over, and (yes, you know what's about to happen) throwing up into the sewer. A late-night bicyclist flew by, trying not to get caught in the wake of the steamy mess freshly deposited on the boulevard. I realized that wasn't that bad of an idea: If someone was sick and ready to throw up in the backseat, simply pull over. "Hell," I said to myself. "If they're drunk, how good could their aim be in a moving car anyway?" thinking about the plastic bags I had provided. I would find out in a few weeks the profound accuracy of that statement.

I believed that for my research to be trustworthy, I had to approach this endeavor as if it were a job. It was my goal to stay on the road until three a.m. that night or $300, whichever came first. On this night, my iPhone buzzed at two forty-five a.m. It was a male name, and I said what the hell. I went to the location, which was a corner on North Avenue between Wicker Park and the Kennedy Expressway. There stood my worst nightmare. He was bone-thin, wearing a black sleeveless T-shirt. Black geometric sleeve tattoos covered his willowy arms, and completing the package were a slick Mohawk haircut and pointed chrome spikes protruding from his nose. *Oh shit*, I thought. I knew in my weekday world I would probably cross the street if this guy were walking toward me. I couldn't just blast by the guy, though, because he would recognize the description of the car and the plate number given to him by Uber. Oh well, here goes.

The guy got in, and I was leery. He asked how my night was going, and I said, "Fine. Yours?" He replied that it was going well and he had just got done working all night in a vegan restaurant. I asked if he had been in that line of work long. He said no and he told me it was just a fill-in job and he was a product tester and wrote reviews for skateboard equipment. He then told me that he was compensated with boxes of T-shirts, for which he then made a good buck by selling them on eBay. He shared with me how his passion for skateboarding took him all over the country and how cool the skateboard people are and how important the rideshare services were to him during his travels. We had a great conversation. On his way out of the car, he told me to be safe. He was a nice kid, following his passion, looking the part, and living the dream. I drove away, putting Dire Straits' "Skateaway" on my iPod, heading home at three a.m.

This had truly been a night to remember, from a petrified young lady to two young women who appeared to have absolutely no inhibitions. I had felt old and almost out of place at points throughout the evening. My aging spirit was brought back to a more soothed state as I recalled my buddy from Iowa and the interesting skateboard entrepreneur. The truth, I told myself, was that these kids were no different than we were as kids. The sad reality is that over the last thirty years, life happened and responsibility took over our spirits. The same will happen for them.

Patrick had had a fun night. Now he was on the balcony amusing himself, reliving the erotic and humorous activities that he had witnessed from a front row seat, howling with laughter. Patrick raised his glass and saluted the prom queens, the general from Des Moines, the lusty Hepburn twins, the vibrator girls, and the inked skateboard tycoon. Pat was exhausted and urged Patrick, the urban raconteur, to get to bed.

THE ART OF CONVERSATION

"Have you been driving Uber long?" "This is the nicest Uber car I've ever been in. Is it yours?" "Are you from Chicago?" "You're not foreign?" That was how a conversation would normally start. Passengers seemed to be fascinated and curious about the driver, and the driver was occasionally curious about the passengers. After I fielded that barrage of questioning, I would get this: "If this is your car, why are you doing this?" I hope I sell as many books as the number of times I was asked that question.

If I wanted to attempt a conversation, I would start asking the questions. "Are you from Chicago?" "Where did you go to school?" "What do you do for a living?" "Where in the area did you grow up?" The depth of the response would indicate to me how detailed a discussion would follow. I could tell who lived alone or had several roommates by the depth and length of their answers. Usually, those who lived alone would be fountains of oration, often sharing with me intimate and uncomfortable aspects of their lives.

When a perfect stranger enters the limited confines of an

automobile, one of two situations occurs. One is an awkward silence, and the other is the beginning of a conversation with an unknown topic dangling at the end of the short journey. Some of the conversations that happened over the three months of driving were insightful, provocative, frustrating, and hilarious. Normally it only took a quick exchange for a passenger to get me to open up or vice versa. The number of substantial conversations I could have in one evening could reach twenty or more. Like on a first date, in one of these conversations, you might find yourself answering the same questions you've answered hundreds of times before. There were certain triggers that could open people up, keeping them talking until the end of the trip. Many times, passengers remained after the meter was off to finish making a point or to finish telling me a story.

On my second or third night driving, a twenty-something man got in the car at roughly seven p.m. I couldn't tell you what he looked like, but I do recall this exchange as the first interesting conversation I had with a fare. We'd been driving for a few minutes, and the young man said to me, "Excuse me, sir. You seem older and like you've been around. Can I ask you a question?"

"Sure, sport," I responded. "What's up?" He asked if I was familiar with "the guy code" (an understanding amongst male friends that they will never date someone that the other has dated in the past). I told him I was. He shared with me that six months after his best friend had broken up with a girl, he himself had started seeing her and they had been having "the best sex ever." Nobody in their close circle of friends knew of their relationship. He was in a dilemma about whether to share this awkward situation with the group, including his buddy. I told him, "I believe that honesty is the best policy, and you might want to tell your buddy first before you do a group *mea culpa*."

He muttered, "But sir, it's the best sex ever." I spent a good ten minutes discussing loyalty and truthfulness. I was starting to feel like a cross between Dr. Phil and Dr. Ruth. Then he said, "Does it matter that she's moving to California tomorrow?" Hell, twenty minutes of hearing about his strong feelings and their great sex, and she was moving. I didn't know what to say.

We arrived at the bar where he was meeting his friends. His partner in the sexual decathlon was not going to be there. She was home packing and he would see her later in the evening. He asked me, "So, what do you think?"

All I could utter, realizing he was not spending the last available night with the love of his life, but instead out drinking with his friends, was, "Best sex ever is tough to pass up."

He looked confused and said, "Yeah, I think I get it." He opened the door, nearly vaulting a fixed-gear cyclist over my rear passenger door. The cyclist regained his composure, steadied his bike, and went on a tirade about lover boy's mother and her indiscriminate sexual habits.

I drove away thinking about what had just happened and wondering what the real message behind his story was. Some friends last a lifetime. How many times has a new sexual partner eclipsed whom you previously thought was the best sexual partner ever? Pat drove away listening to Patsy Cline's "Crazy."

Not all discussions involved relationships or were long-winded. Often, I would drive while listening to passengers talk among themselves. Two young men in particular stick in my memory for two reasons. First, they were having a good conversation on a topic that I'm fairly well versed in. Second, I had fun with them at the end of the ride. They were both young stock option traders and were spiritedly debating what their next moves in the stock option market should be. Understandably, to them, I was an old man pushing iron for roughly

$20 an hour. In one of my many past lives, however, I had worked on the Chicago Board Options Exchange, and I had participated in the investment industry for well over fifteen years. Also, I still trade stock options for my own account regularly.

One of the men was concerned that the market might correct but was hesitant that he might miss more potential upside gains. The other man was worried about the summer doldrums in the stock market and that the market might not move much. The debate was well constructed and articulated. Their concerns over the economy and what moves the Federal Reserve might make were thrown back and forth. They had additional concerns over the brutal weather that the country had experienced in the first three months of the year. What would the GDP (Gross Domestic Product) be, given the harsh spring weather, one fretted out loud. All their concerns were valid.

They continued to go back and forth, playing out potential scenarios with the S&P 500, with no definite outcome. These poor guys were going out on Friday night for fun, and they were in no way in the mood for frolicking. I had not said a word. I was just the old man in the white T-shirt and the blue cardigan sweater. Two minutes away from their destination, I chirped, "If I had to be long but wanted to keep some powder dry, I would buy the SPY August 180 calls and sell the SPY August 200 call against them. If I was concerned about the doldrums, I would sell the SPY September 180 straddle." These are both stock option strategies.

When I pulled up in front of the bar, their mouths were open in disbelief. I had to do it. It was too tempting. I told them to have fun, and I drove away listening to 10cc's "Wall Street Shuffle."

Not all conversations have good outcomes. Some can have ugly endings. On the first weekend of the Gay Pride Festival, I picked up four young girls in Lincoln Park. They gave me an address on

Broadway, and I was off to Boystown again. It was about eleven-thirty p.m., and the street was mobbed, so traffic was barely moving. The girls occasionally asked me questions. They were from a Big Ten school and were loaded for bear. One asked if it bothered me to go into that neighborhood, and I said absolutely not. They were trying to get me to that political area that I didn't like to enter with passengers. I'm a person who likes to research all points of view pertaining to a subject and draw an informed conclusion before making a decision. The topic they peppered me with questions about was a topic I had not researched thoroughly and had not formed an opinion on one way or the other. They asked me what my position was on gay marriage.

I replied, "I'm not sure, but I'm in favor of the civil union—" Before I could finish my answer, the passenger in the front seat demanded that I stop the car and let them out. I did. They slammed my car doors and left the vehicle. If I had been able to finish my answer, Pat would have said, "I'm not sure, but I'm in favor of the civil union because of a dear friend..." His friend was as much a confidant and an advisor to Pat as Pat was to him. Pat remembered his concerns around health care and wealth distribution with his life partner of many years long before the civil union was recognized in this country.

The young lady also didn't know that in the early 1980s, when I was a stockbroker, I sat with a young client who was planning his niece's and nephew's college funds from his life insurance proceeds as a new disease ravaged his young body and mind. When we finished our work, we sat together, we had a drink together, and we cried together. *Who is this child to pass judgment on me?* Pat angrily thought. Pat thought about their reaction, and he reminded himself, *Children know what they see. Is that not how our political parties deal with each other?*

Patrick mumbled to himself, "Fucking little bitches." Civil debate and enlightening exchange of ideas are a lost art in this country. I drove away listening to Mott the Hoople's "All the Young Dudes."

One night I picked up three young ladies and a guy on Hubbard Street. He sat in front, and they sat in the backseat. They started with the usual litany of questions. I decided to fire back and ask them what they did for a living. They all quickly responded that they were in the advertising business. Patrick turned to the young guy in the front seat and pried, "So, are you the Don Draper of the firm?" (Don Draper is the fictional womanizing advertising executive from the television series *Mad Men*.)

As soon as I asked that, one young lady in the backseat yelled, "Does that mean you're going to put your penis in me?" I laughed, as did everybody else in the car. She certainly broke the ice on this short trip. They asked me about the wildest thing I had experienced. Seeing that this ride was a few weeks before the infamous dueling vibrator twins, the shock level was still climbing. Patrick shared with the young, eager riders the story about the young lady trying to coerce her boyfriend to spend the night at her place by offering "that special thing" he liked.

As soon I relayed "special thing," a pretty, but plain-looking, girl blurted out, "You mean butt sex?"

The other two ladies in the backseat cracked up and said, "No, we think she meant oral gratification."

All bets were off on this ride, and I had no idea how bizarre this night was going to be. The guy and the quiet girl got dropped off first, and I was left with the two outgoing girls with highly revved libidos in the backseat. They lived very close to one another, so they were going to get out at the same location. I pulled up to the address and turned off the meter on the iPhone. The girl sitting behind me wanted to know if she could ask my opinion on something. I replied, "Sure. Why not?" After the butt sex outburst, what could be a more shocking question?

The events of the next ten minutes would force me to reach down to the accelerator pedal and lift my jaw off the floor.

She explained to me that she had always kept herself shaved in a very private region and that was the only way her boyfriend had ever seen her. They were going to a wedding at the end of the summer, and she wanted to get a full Brazilian wax treatment. To get her Brazilian, she had to let the hair in that region grow out. (At this point, I was nodding as if someone were telling me how to prepare a meal or change a tire. Yes, yes, so nonchalantly I nodded.) Her concern was that while she prepared for her Brazilian, she didn't want to gross him out. She looked at me as seriously as a heart attack victim and asked, "Do you think me having a bush will turn him off and make him not interested in having sex with me?"

Patrick thought for a minute and replied, as seriously as he possibly could without losing it, "It didn't retard the growth of the human race dating back to the cavemen days up and through the decade of the eighties. I think you will be alright for a few weeks." We were sitting in front of her apartment, having a nice conversation about female genitalia, and we had just met thirty minutes before.

Her fellow passenger had a question too. This was the young lady who had blurted out the butt sex question. First, she asked her friend who had hair concerns if she waxed or bleached in the back. I was nodding as if we were discussing the Blackhawks' chances in the playoffs. (For the record, she waxed there, too.) Then the second girl shared with us that she was having penetration issues with that special back door act she was apparently so fixated on. She asked me if I had any suggestions. All I could say, in a startled, yet very tired way was, "It's like anything else. Practice makes perfect."

Ms. Brazilian had a few angle suggestions, and they continued to share the challenges of sex in the twenty-first century. It was close to two a.m., and when I started to talk with a German accent like Dr. Ruth, I knew it was time to end the question-and-answer period. I drove into the night, shaking my head and uttering to myself yet again, "No one is going to believe this shit," while listening to Crosby, Stills, Nash and Young's "Almost Cut My Hair."

Sometimes, the truth hurts—and if you ask me an honest question, I will give you an honest answer.

I picked up a family. Mom and Dad were in their fifties and had that fresh-off-the-country-club look. Their two children were in their twenties. Mom and Dad were from Ohio, visiting their daughter in Chicago. The daughter lived in the West Loop, and they were headed to dinner near Water Tower Place. It was roughly six-thirty p.m., and traffic was slow. The wife asked me questions about Hi Ho. "What year is your car?" she asked. "What options does the car have?" I was truthful and answered her questions.

She then asked how much I liked the car. "Well, I've owned over seventy cars, and eight of them have been Mercedes-Benzes, but I'm not pleased with this model. This car, for some reason, is the worst of the lot. It's had nothing but computer issues." She continued to probe, and I pointed out to her that every light and code was illuminated on my dash. I nicely said, "Lady, all these colorful lights on my dash aren't Christmas decorations. They're supposed to be warning me of system failures, and every time I go to my mechanic and he plugs the car into the diagnostic computer, it shows there's nothing wrong." I then told her how expensive it can be if one of the many computer-operated functions on the car failed.

I commented on how refreshing it was to have a passenger so interested in cars. Looking in the rearview mirror, I could see the poor lady's face. She looked like someone had just told her that she had to put her dog down. She looked up and sadly said, "I just bought one of these the day before I left for Chicago. I always wanted a Mercedes-Benz."

I tried to backtrack and explain that mine could be an exception and her car would be great. Then Skippy, her husband, in the blue blazer, kelly green pants, and penny loafers without socks, said, "Damn it, Marge, I told you to get the Audi." I felt like such a schmuck. The car was quiet for the remainder of the ride. We arrived at the restaurant, and this guy gave me a ten-dollar tip. He was one of only three people out of the hundreds of rides to give me a cash tip. He probably felt sorry for me with my car-repair bills.

Driving away, I listened to—what else? —Janis Joplin's "Mercedes Benz."

Rarely did I get passengers over forty years of age. My age and the fact that I was driving Uber did not mean I was a disgruntled Baby Boomer angry about the state of the country and his unachieved dreams. Granted, I'm not pleased with several issues, but I'm not an extremist in either direction. One night I picked up a couple in their early sixties. They were in town visiting their daughter and grandchildren. Their daughter buzzed Uber for them, and I picked them up in Lincoln Park and headed to a downtown hotel. Pops started out on the younger, entitled generation and how they were all no good.

Wow, that's harsh right out of the box, I thought. *I have two pretty decent hardworking sons at home.*

Pops went on to rip on the Millennial generation as being "those entitled, hedonistic young brats who have their noses in computers and gadgets."

The negative diatribe continued for a good ten minutes while Patrick thought, *Does this fossil realize what's facilitating his ride to the hotel? Or that the application that fuels this economical mode of transportation was probably written by a fifteen-year-old millionaire?* I kept my mouth shut and let him continue.

While we were waiting at a light, an attractive young lady in yoga pants crossed the street in front of the car. He growled, "Disgusting. They all dress like whores."

Pat couldn't take it anymore and asked him, "Weren't we the Woodstock generation? Didn't many of the women of our generation shed their bras and walk with bouncing breasts with their nipples extended?"

He didn't like that question. "Not where I come from, pal," he retorted. Pat figured it was best to shut up and focus on driving the car because neither the passenger nor Pat needed a coronary. Also, I realized that this clown's level of tolerance was no different than that of the little debate queen who wouldn't let me finish my answer regarding gay marriage. I surmised that U.S.A. might stand for "usual stereotypical assumptions." I wondered if maybe we might all get along better if we limited our communications to texting each other. That way the raw, emotional response might not be as biting.

We pulled up to the hotel, and the rider asked how he paid for the ride. I turned to look at him and said, "It's a frictionless transaction all done by a computer," and smiled and nodded. Even in this world of technology and rapid data movement, nothing is as pleasing or destructive as the word, spoken or unspoken.

That night as I drove home, my mind and soul bore the pain of the evening more than my back and legs. I thought about how we communicate with each other and the value we place on our freedom of speech as a society. We're in the age of hundreds of "friends" on social media, instantaneous communication, and even on-demand video chat, but we fail to listen to one another. The exchange of ideas and the concept of even attempting to truly hear an opposite point of view are lost. A well-crafted debate, where both sides have researched and are passionate about their points of view, is a jewel of the human intellect. Maybe if we limit our arguments to 140 characters, use acronyms, and find a way to radiate emojis through our eyes, we can still share different and opposite points of view. I considered my life and realized I've learned so much from listening to those who did not necessarily agree with my point of view. *What happened to the art of conversation?* I wondered as I drove away, staring into space and listening to Pink Floyd's "Comfortably Numb."

Back on the balcony of discontent with four fingers of scotch and a pack of Marlboros in hand, Pat was deeply troubled and feeling hurt when he thought about the four girls who had stormed out of the car. Patrick still felt he should have put the window down and told her to go fuck herself. The usual Pat and Patrick evening summation argument had begun. Patrick also wanted a crack at the argumentative old man. He told Pat, *We could have taken him*. Pat just rolled his eyes in disgust. Then Pat thought about the young options traders and questioned why the hell he was doing this and how he was going to embarrass himself by writing a book. Patrick was chuckling about his "Brazilian" friend and the young girl blurting out "butt sex." It was all getting to be too much stimulation in a short period of time for Pat. Pat dragged his lifeless right leg up the stairs to his bedroom while the loud voices of the night still reverberated in his embattled head.

20 OUT OF
48 HOURS

The summer in Chicago has many milestone events that mark its brief season, from Greek, Italian, German, Middle Eastern, and other ethnic festivals to barbeque competitions, the Gay Pride Festival, art fairs, hamburger cook-offs, outdoor concerts, Lollapalooza, and A Taste of Chicago. The city also hosts two major league baseball teams, as well as tourist attractions too numerous to list. Chicago attracts more than forty-six million tourists and conventioneers every year. The natives play sixteen-inch softball, golf, tennis, playground basketball, and even beach volleyball. The roads are inundated with joggers and cyclists. The end of June and the beginning of July are the shank of the summer season in Chicago.

Summer is also the season of road and bridge repair in our city. The road crews close traffic lanes, often diverting drivers to a pothole-ridden lane or a partially repaired lane with sewer covers that rise three to four inches above grade. A GPS is rendered useless when confronted with a road repair detour. These are a few of the practical issues and challenges of rideshare driving in a Windy City summer.

It was the last week of June, and the city's agenda was again packed. Neighborhood festivals were clogging streets all over the city, from Rogers Park to Bridgeport, barricading routes and forcing undesirable alternatives. Then there's the person summoning an Uber while standing in the middle of a festival, inaccessible and three blocks away from a driver. Needless to say, this can create a great deal of confusion and pissed off riders, as well as drivers.

The outside temperature was reaching extreme local norms, and as the car idled in a road repair delay, the engine was forced to function in high heat while the air conditioning robbed the fuel tank at a more expensive pace. I noticed that the front suspension had begun to rattle like four denture-wearing octogenarians casually eating peanuts.

On Friday, June 27, 2014, at six p.m., the car was full of gas, the Taser was charged, and it was time to roll. I turned on the iPhone, and within two minutes, a buzz came from a bar on Lincoln Avenue. I was stuck in traffic because an elderly driver in a Jag sedan had brushed the rear wheel of a bicycle at the intersection, and the bike rider wouldn't leave the intersection, blocking the old guy in until the police arrived. I was close to the bar when the ride canceled.

As I drove east, heading to North Avenue, the same fare buzzed me to the same address. I pulled a U-turn and headed back up Lincoln Avenue. When I was within a block of the bar, the customer canceled again. I was starting to get a bit upset. I pulled another U-turn and headed back to North Avenue. Again, I got to the intersection of North and Lincoln and the fare buzzed me to the same location. Again, I pulled another U-turn and headed back up Lincoln Avenue. I was extremely pissed off. Arriving at the bar, I hit the button announcing my arrival, then I angrily waited.

Pat was fuming as his flashers ticked and no one appeared. Then, I heard a pounding on the rear window. I heard a voice yelling, "Hey, dude, you Uber?" Three young Middle-Eastern–American men got in the car, beyond buzzed. They were, as we said in the seventies, fucked up. They were all wearing baseball hats with the holograph stickers still affixed and oversized basketball shorts representing various college basketball powers. One of the guys sat in the front seat and said, "Hi, Patrick. We've been celebrating my twenty-first birthday since eleven this morning. Get us to Water Tower Place, dude." I looked at him, still pissed about the three U-turns in rush hour. He looked at me and said, "You don't look happy, dude." Patrick asked what the hell was up with the repeated cancelations. He replied, "Sorry, man. We kept doing shots."

This did not help my mood. The heavyset fella sitting directly behind me chimed in, "This is a fine ride, man. Do you have FM radio in here? Come on, man. A Benz has to have FM. I want a certain station."

Normally, if the passenger is nice, Pat will try to accommodate, but Patrick told him, "We're listening to satellite radio. Enjoy." Before I knew it, the birthday boy started playing with the radio controls. I still can't believe what I did.

Patrick looked at him in a snarky manner, gently slapped the back of the passenger's hand as if he were a five-year-old, and said, "Do not touch."

This prompted Chubby to say, "Hey, bro, you have to chill. Pull over and do a bong and a line with us."

I laughed, looked in the rearview mirror, thanked him for his generous offer, and said, "No thanks." Then I decided to have a little fun. Hell, they were driving me nuts with delays, music, and their assessment of my attitude. Patrick asked them if he could stop at police headquarters and pick up his paycheck because he was off duty that day. The blood left their faces.

I looked in the mirror. "Hey, bro, you have to chill out. I was just messing with you." They all managed a nervous laugh. Birthday Boy was a little freaked out and became quiet.

When we pulled up to Water Tower Place, they exited a little more quickly than they had entered the car. I smiled and said, "Happy birthday," with a grin. I drove away listening to—what else—the Police's "Walking on the Moon."

That first ride of my weekend was an omen of what was yet to come.

I was on north Michigan Avenue at seven-thirty, weaving through traffic, feeling aggressive. I was getting early evening commuters in a hurry to get to the train to flee the city for the weekend. Slowly I migrated north and ended up in Lincoln Park again. The next buzz came from a stately brownstone on Fullerton.

Right away, a young girl of about fourteen and a boy who appeared to be twelve came down the stairs. They both had reddish-orange hair and freckled faces, and were smartly, but casually, dressed. The girl asked if I knew where the Cineplex was on Clybourn Avenue. I said yes. She then asked, "Can you get us there briskly? We're going to try and have dinner before we go to the movie." I replied that I would try. She turned to the boy, who, I surmised, was her younger brother, because they looked very much alike. She said to him, "Joshua, I cannot believe I acquiesced to eating Thai food tonight, seeing that I had sushi with Allyson for lunch." *Hmm,* I thought, *pity the maid that gives this kid a peanut butter and jelly sandwich for lunch someday.* Joshua then listed the menu choices, and they debated the time they had for the food to be prepared before the movie began. Joshua was adamant that they order nothing containing ginger. They recited the menu from memory, and they made their decisions ahead of time.

They were very courteous and somewhat cute in their manner. We arrived at the intersection of Clybourn and Wrightwood. They thanked me very much and were off to have pad thai and spring rolls. I sat in the car for a minute and I reflected that in one hour, I had gone from being invited to do a bong and a line with the Arabian Knights to feeling like Mr. French dropping Buffy and Jody off for dinner and a movie. I then hoped my book about this journey would sell, because the therapy from all of this was going to be expensive. Driving away, I listened to 10,000 Maniacs' "My Sister Rose."

The night was fairly normal. Destinations included bars, restaurants, bowling alleys, and theaters. I was cruising through a boring night for a weekend, but as usual, a new experience was right around the corner. A buzz came, and after I responded my phone rang. (There is a mechanism that allows fares to call me without me knowing their phone number or they mine.) A male voice asked if I was the Uber driver responding to the call. I said yes and asked how I could I help him. He told me he had a special request. He wanted me to pick up a young lady at a certain location, drive her to Orland Park, Illinois, where I would wait an hour, and then return to the address of origin. I thought about it, and I realized that Orland Park was roughly thirty miles from Chicago and that with the one-hour wait, this would be a $200 trip.

Agreeing to the arrangement, I proceeded to the address. When I arrived, I called the man back, and he said he would tell her I was waiting. After ten minutes, a beautiful, long-legged, dark-haired woman in her mid-twenties entered my car. She was very pleasant, and she talked about general topics all the way out to Orland Park. The GPS guided me to a dark road set back in what appeared to be thick woods. My high beams helped me navigate the winding road. Finally, we arrived at a large home with several expensive vehicles in the driveway. The fat, balding gentleman waved from the door, and the young lady exited the car. He instructed me to keep the meter running and to go get something to eat. Then I was to come back in an hour. I knew what was going on. She was an escort, and I was driving her. Another new experience I could keep off the resumé.

I ate breakfast at a twenty-four-hour joint and I gassed up the car, which killed an hour. I went back to the house and waited in the horseshoe-shaped driveway. After thirty minutes, my phone rang. The mystery man asked that I keep the meter on and wait another hour. What was I going to say? I waited. It was approaching two a.m. I decided to recline the seat and get paid to nap. An hour later, the phone rang, and again, I acquiesced for yet another hour. Then I dug in for an uncomfortable nap.

Finally, at four-thirty in the morning, the young lady returned to the car. Her hair was mussed, and gone was the friendly demeanor that she had had on the trip out. She handed me an envelope and said, "Get me home."

I opened the envelope. Inside were two crisp one hundred dollar bills. This cash plus the meter being on all night made this a $500 excursion. I was tired and not feeling very comfortable about my passenger, who now looked tussled and smelled extremely foul. Unable to speed because the only other cars on the road seemed to be police cars, I thought this could be a difficult situation to explain. My passenger was quiet. As the sky began to lighten I found my way back to the highway, praying I would not take out a deer. She was quiet as I approached the highway, and I thought the worst was over.

After we had been on the highway for five minutes, her phone rang. It was four forty-five in the morning. I was focused on the road and just wanted to get home. I heard her say, "Bruce, the banquet ended late and we had to clean up the banquet hall." She also told him that the wait staff could not carry cell phones, which was why she had not answered the twenty calls he had placed during the evening.

I could hear the guy screaming that he didn't believe her, and he wanted to know exactly where she was and who the hell was driving her home. *Shit, will I be driving into an ambush?* Pat wondered. The argument grew in intensity, and I was getting concerned that this was going to be ugly when I finally got her home. The funniest part of this argument was when she said to this guy at five a.m. after being out all night and not receiving his cell calls, "Bruce, you have trust issues." *I guess he does*, Patrick thought. Pat wondered if anyone still tells the truth.

We left the expressway on the Near West Side. I was still trying to obey every traffic law because we were quite conspicuous in this neighborhood at this time of the morning in this car. To make it worse, she was in the backseat. Finally, I turned right on her street, my tired eyes darting left to right, up and down, repeatedly scanning for old trust-issues Brucey. *Is this my Little Big Horn?* I wondered. Luckily, he had not yet arrived. She left the car, and Hi Ho flew out of that neighborhood. I was gone before she hit the curb.

I was downtown. There was not a soul on the streets in the financial district. It was peaceful and surreal to be there at that time of morning. I decided to take Lake Shore Drive home. Watching the morning lights rise over this tremendous city with the lake to my right was awe-inspiring. The sun began to force its way through the clouds, and the sounds of the birds in the quiet city, which is normally loud and crowded, were amazing. I drove in silence, but for the soothing sounds of the birds. Pat thought about the beauty and ugliness of this night, the diversity of the people he drove, and the city that he loved roaming. Shaken by boldface lies told in the back of his car, he was angered by the lack of courtesy from a person who thought they could soothe him with money after keeping him out all night sleeping in a strange driveway. At the same time, he was filled with pride and admiration for the early morning beauty and the aesthetic wonder that was his hometown. Yet the majesty of this great sleeping city gave Pat little hope. As his mind raced, he remembered a quote from Socrates: "Hope, the solace of old age, is ever present." Man, did Pat crave hope. He then focused on that thought and his mind drifted to the health and welfare of the gentleman in the tweed cap and beige golf jacket.

I woke up at two in the afternoon, stiff and hurting following my night of driveway snoozing. This was the stiffest and most painful Saturday I had during the entire experience. I ate breakfast, chased it with a handful of aspirin, and then realized that I had been behind the wheel of the car for well over twelve hours the day before. I decided to get the car washed and come home to a nap before heading back to the late-night asphalt obstacle course.

While I was getting the car washed, I gazed into space and thought of the stranger I had dropped off before sunrise. I wondered if her friend on the phone had ever calmed down. When the car was done, the same guy who had confronted me about the two joints in the backseat waved me over to come see him again. *Now what?* I thought. He looked at me and said, "Señor, this was left in the backseat of your car." It was a small, brown vial the same color and size as the vial that contains the nitro pills my cardiologist prescribes for me in case of chest pains. But this was not nitro. There was a white powder residue in the bottle. Knowing what it was, and remembering the episode with my three buddies celebrating a twenty-first birthday, there was no doubt where it came from. This little gift was my payback. At that point, I knew paybacks could be a bitch. I asked the kind fella at the car wash if he could dispose of the vial. I decided that for the next few weeks, it might be best to find a new car wash, because I didn't want to find the DEA waiting for me at the end of the car wash line.

At six-thirty p.m., I was back on the road, aching and tired, but true to my mission. A quick buzz came from a Lincoln Park address, where two nice young men got in. They were flight attendants in their late thirties. We had a great conversation about airline safety and the sensitive nature of being in a service industry. I dropped them off at a bar on Broadway and realized that Boystown was extremely busy at this early hour, that the crowds were substantially more animated than usual. The pace was consistent, and I was shuttling people to the active strip of bars on Broadway for a good two hours. Then, a buzz returned me to Lincoln Park. Off I went to another mystery fare, fighting rush-hour automobile traffic and bicycle congestion.

I arrived at a beautiful Lincoln Park greystone. Because it was after eight, I was expecting another excited reveler. Looking up, I saw a woman who had to be over sixty approaching, and I unlocked the car. She got in and gave me an address on the Southwest Side, so off we went. She said, "Sir, this is the nicest car I've ever been in." I smiled and said thank you. She went on to explain that she was a nanny for four young children and she normally left work at five, but today she had to work late because of her missus having company in from out of town. She told me that this was her boss's Uber account and that she normally took a bus and an 'L' home, but tonight, because of the late hour, her boss had treated her to a ride home. Again, she softly stated that this was "the most wonderful car" she had ever been in and that she "felt like a princess." Hi Ho was blushing.

I asked what kind of music she liked. She answered jazz, so I found a jazz station and told her, "Put your feet up and enjoy the ride home, princess." When we reached her house, she thanked me profusely. As I drove away enjoying Dave Brubeck's "Take Five" on the satellite channel, I thought about all the things that many of us take for granted.

A buzz came from a nearby bar, and I picked up a couple who

wanted to go to Hyde Park, a beautiful and culturally diverse section of the city that is home to the University of Chicago. They were discussing their final exams and plans for the summer. After I dropped them off on campus, I made my way east to Lake Shore Drive. As I made my way through the campus streets, my mind wandered to Hyde Park history. My first thought was that the atomic bomb had been built under a football field a few blocks away. Next, my attention turned to the man crossing the street in a summer tweed sport coat with a number of newspapers under his arm. Could he possibly be a Nobel Prize winner? It was at that point Pat realized that during the week he was constantly thinking about the events of his Uber weekend, but while driving he never thinks about the significant business issues that occur Monday through Friday.

Driving through leafy, green Hyde Park leading to northbound Lake Shore Drive, my mind shifted to the Leopold and Loeb murder case. Two men in their twenties had murdered a ten-year-old boy in the 1920s. This was a dark, yet fascinating, piece of the neighborhood's and the city's history. These two young men thought they had planned and executed the perfect crime. What they hadn't realized was that one of the murderers had dropped a pair of eyeglasses with a spring hinge that had been newly invented by a young Chicago ophthalmologist, Elmer Coe. Because only three pairs of these frames were in circulation, identifying the murderers was easy.

When the car was empty, the random train of thoughts stimulated by the city of my birth was endless. I headed back downtown, being careful not to get a speeding ticket on northbound Lake Shore Drive and listening to Jackson Browne's "Doctor My Eyes."

Wicker Park was very busy. I was stuck in the neighborhood, but the work was fast and easy. A buzz came from a bar west of Wicker Park on Milwaukee Avenue. I couldn't find my rider because all the bars were spilling patrons onto the streets. It was around midnight, and I had missed my pickup, so I decided to turn down an alley ten feet past a crowd of roughly seventy-five young people waiting to get into a club. Immediately on entering the alley, I stopped in amazement. At least five hundred rats were playing in the alley like fourth-graders who had just been released for the summer. I detest rats, but I'm the type of person who gets bummed for a few minutes if I accidently hit a squirrel or a rabbit with my car.

Looking at the potential carnage bound by overflowing dumpsters, I decided what to do. I came to grips with the fact that below this city was another city, where the inhabitants had four legs, carried diseases, and had tails. We coexist with millions of these nasty critters, but they have learned how to hide in plain sight. "Time to do Rahm, the Mayor of Chicago, a favor," Patrick said, and he went hunting for vermin. He put the car in neutral, revved the engine, and dropped the gear shift into drive. The rats scattered with unbelievable speed and agility, but I heard at least five thuds under the car's floorboards. In my journal I made an entry to make sure to pay extra to wash the undercarriage. Then I turned right on the side street and then again on Milwaukee Avenue and found my fare waiting in sandals. I thought it best not to share with her the exciting discovery I had made ten feet from where she was flaunting her freshly pedicured toes in gladiator-style sandals.

This night was going by quickly and it was relatively calm for a Saturday. It was well after one in the morning when I stopped at the doughnut shop to refuel with coffee and a muffin. My plan was to push to after three a.m. I turned the Uber phone back on and was quickly summoned back to Wicker Park. Passing the address on Damen Avenue, I realized I had to be on the other side of the street, so I pulled one of my many U-turns of the evening. I pulled up to the bar, and a young lady was waiting. She started to get in, when out of nowhere, a guy grabbed the door behind her. He was upset and stuck his head in the car, yelling, "I thought you were calling a taxi. This is no taxi. Is this the guy you're fucking?"

She tried to explain the rideshare concept and that I was an Uber driver. I couldn't believe how calm I was as this idiot continued to force his head and shoulders into my car, trying to position himself to take a swing meant for some unknown lover. My little electric friend was cocked in my left hand, and I calmly said, "Hey, pal, do you see all this electronic equipment up here?" Pat was pointing to the iPhone and the GPS. "This is an Uber vehicle." Pat explained it to him as he seethed. Then Pat said, "Unless she has a daddy fetish, I seriously doubt I'm your carnal competition." He stopped and looked at the electronic gear in the car. Then, not to put too fine a point on it, Patrick said, "Now get the fuck out of my car."

He walked away, she stayed. I drove her home. I felt a warrior bravado radiating from my glare. Patrick was a warrior with an AARP card, blended-lens bifocals, and a nitro prescription. Not a word was said on the drive, and she left the car to walk slowly to her apartment. Driving away, I was in disbelief of how calm I was compared to how I had been in the similar incident a few weeks before. I drove listening to Tom Petty's "I Won't Back Down."

It was approaching two a.m. I was totally unfazed by what had just happened. The iPhone buzzed me to a frequently patronized watering hole on Wells Street. Three guys in their mid-twenties entered the car. They seemed cool, and the one behind me requested 18th and Indiana. *Damn*, I thought, because I did not want to head south at this time of night. We headed for Lake Shore Drive south, and the guy behind me asked, "What's up with the ride?" I smiled and told him I was writing a book about being a rideshare driver. "Nice," he replied. I looked in the mirror and saw a red-faced guy with the map of Ireland across his mug wearing a pristine 1984 Chicago White Sox baseball cap. He was with his buds in more ways than one, and he was feeling good.

He asked me to share with him some of the anecdotes that would be in the book. I humored him with a few stories, and his response blew my mind. "That book sounds good. I'll have to illegally download it when it comes out. You know, guys, I haven't read anything since *Mad Magazine* in high school," he cheerfully chirped. I loved the honesty and candor about the illegal download. He viewed his corrupt interest as a compliment. I drove away listening to Eric Burdon's "Spill the Wine."

The late night brings out either very quiet passengers or extremely loud groups heading home. I had a few mundane trips and again I was sent to Old Town. Two young women in their early thirties wearing jeans and T-shirts got in the car. They were friendly and in a good mood. They were talking to each other and occasionally chatting with me. My iPod played softly. One of the ladies asked me to put it louder. We were headed north on Lake Shore Drive, and I wasn't paying attention to what music was playing. I turned up the iPod and heard Jerry Lee Lewis belt out "Great Balls of Fire." Both started to sing and dance as if they were at a high school dance. They opened their windows and yelled the words of the song for all to hear. They were elevating off the seats, jiggling, wiggling, and having a damn good time.

The next song was by Jerry Lee Lewis as well—"Whole Lotta Shaking Going On," and the intensity of the dancing and singing went up another level. One of them yelled out, "Come on, Patrick, hit the gas pedal and let's have some fun." They were two fun young mothers making the most of a weekend ladies' night out. It was simply cool. When I dropped them off, they thanked me for a great ride. I thanked them as well, and then I drove away in needed silence.

I enjoyed the fact that two strangers had ended their night out having a good time in my car. It was after three and I had spent twenty of the past forty-eight hours either driving or napping behind the wheel of my car. I had responded to more than forty-five ride requests and I had driven more than one hundred strangers. My mind remembered many of the voices and very few faces. Laughing, I thought about illegally downloading my yet-to-be-completed book. I thought of the young lady walking from the car alone after the crazed guy had accused her of infidelity and had embarrassed her in front of me. I wondered if any other rideshare driver was sleeping in a driveway in Orland Park tonight, and if my female passenger from four-thirty this morning was at another "banquet."

My right leg was pulsating as I pressed the brake pedal on the way home that early Sunday morning. Voices from the weekend rang in Pat's ears, professing their falsehoods. Pat would shudder at the number of times the first passenger would leave the car, giving me his date's address, but as soon as the door closed, his date would direct me elsewhere. Lies from people on the phone in the backseat about where they were and with whom—they were all played out for Pat, the invisible spectator. This was starting to affect him in a severely negative way. Pat's trust level of even people he loved was swiftly deteriorating. His mind could not balance the wave of deceit that bombarded him every weekend. As I slowly removed my aching carcass from the front seat of the car, I realized that in twenty of the past forty-eight hours, I had seen all that is ugly and all that is beautiful about people coexisting in a densely populated urban environment.

That night both Pat and Patrick were way too tired for the balcony. They poured a glass of milk and, with the aid of the banister, painfully hobbled upstairs where they crashed on the bed.

LOVE A PARADE

June 29, 2014, was a day circled on the calendars of gay and straight men and women throughout the Midwest. The Chicago event with its pageantry, outfits, floats, politicians, music, alcohol, and flamboyancy resembles Mardi Gras in New Orleans. It was the Gay Pride Parade, the culmination of the annual Gay Pride Festival, held on Broadway, a few blocks east of Wrigley Field. Public transportation was jammed, and certain streets were barricaded with light blue, wooden traffic horses as thousands of people crammed into a one-mile-long strip of the city. I decided to take a pass on the early day rush to the parade because I knew this event had a history of lingering into the late night and early morning of the next day.

At four in the afternoon, I decided to venture out and fight the forces. I headed east down Belmont and was quickly buzzed to a local address. A young man with a beard entered the car and he gave me an address on Broadway. Where else? He didn't look excited to be headed in that direction, but it wasn't any of my business. As traffic ground to a standstill, he mumbled, "I'm gay, but I hate this week." I looked up into the mirror and asked why. He explained that Gay Pride Week attracts the worst element of the gay community. I didn't say much as he explained why he was dreading the next eight hours of bartending in the middle of the spectacle.

The best I could do was get him to within three blocks of his destination. He left the car and walked the remainder of the distance. He was a nice guy getting ready to purvey liquor to the proud masses.

Traffic crawled, and before I knew it, I was stuck on Broadway. There were police on every corner and ambulances trying to move in every direction. I was amazed that even hours after the floats, politicians, and bands had dispersed, thousands of people were still partying and milling around the neighborhood. The well-defined street and sidewalk boundaries no longer existed. The police were congregated in groups of four to ten on every corner. You could see the perspiration from the men and women in blue as they stood in the sun, sporting their communication devices and heavy equipment belts. They looked tired, but most were smiling and looking away from mildly offensive behavior. The ambulances were filled with over-served and under-hydrated parade-goers. The sidewalks and streets were filled with colorful and provocatively dressed people of all ages, garbed in everything from leather codpieces to extravagant evening gowns. There were men holding hands and women kissing each other. There were people of all shapes, sizes, and colors demonstrating happiness and pride.

I had been sitting still on Broadway for at least a half-hour. My phone buzzed, and I began to laugh. *How the hell can I go anywhere?* I thought as I rejected the call, realizing that we were in a five-times-normal-fare bonus period. The phone buzzed again, and the icon that signifies passenger location was right on the car. I looked up as two extremely heavyset African-American men in dresses and colorful hats entered the car. Their masculine feet bulged over the sides of their tasteful pumps like bread dough rising over the lip of a bowl. They gave me an address in the South Loop, and we continued to idle. It was taking us thirty minutes to travel one city block. They weren't talking to me, but were pointing at the outfits on people in the street and on the sidewalk and waving when they saw someone they knew. They were excited.

My eyes immediately focused on one person, a gorgeous woman crossing the street, a tall, high-cheek-boned African-American goddess. Her hair was done up high, her skirt slit even higher, and she looked as if she stepped right off a Las Vegas chorus line. She knew she was hot, and that the majority of eyes were upon her. As she stepped off the curb, forcing her right leg to open the high slit of her gown, she showed the adoring crowd her man bits flopping from side to side. I looked and said to myself, "What came first, the chicken or the egg?"

As we sat, stuck in traffic, I marveled at the stream of incredible outfits. Two men, one white and the other Hispanic, each one at least 350 pounds, were wearing nothing but brassieres and pink tutus. The guys in my car became very excited and lowered the window, yelling hello to the men they referred to as Tony and Jeremy. I looked in the other direction and spied a guy sporting a yellow banana suit. Looking back the other way, I saw a woman with her beaded breasts out, swinging in all directions.

We had not moved an inch, and one of my passengers complained about the traffic situation. The other guy told me that increased fares were a direct attack by the rideshare industry against the gay community. *Why is everything in this society a conspiracy against a protected class?* Pat thought. He didn't say a word, but had to admit it was a bit different, taking shit from two guys dressed like his grandmother.

We had moved a block and a half, and my nostrils noticed that the undersized pumps had been removed, for comfort, no doubt. The men had now been in the car forty minutes and were becoming abusive. One of them asked me what the fare was at that point, but I didn't know. There was no visible meter with the Uber program like in a taxi. It wasn't possible to know until the ride was complete. If I could get to a side street that was not barricaded, I could take an alternate route, but I was stuck in suffocating traffic in the midst of a wild party. One of the passengers sat on the edge of the rear seat and leaned towards me. "You. I am talking to you. What are you going to do about this predicament you got us into?"

The other chimed in, "He's nothing but a meter thief."

Patrick had reached his boiling point, so he turned to them and said, "You can sit back in that seat. I don't need you breathing down my neck. As for your predicament, this is not my goddamn parade, and I have not created this congestion. Hey, Thelma and Louise, why don't you take your six-inch heels and sashay your fat asses down the street on your feet for free?"

They left, slamming the door. I turned off the iPhone. The bill came to $28 for going less than two blocks. "Oops," I said as Hi Ho continued to idle in traffic. I listened to David Bowie's "Suffragette City."

Traffic finally moved enough to allow me to turn off Broadway and be released from the Twilight Zone. Before the car hit Fullerton Avenue, the iPhone buzzed. Two tall, blond, and ripped young men got into the car. Really, these two guys were really tall. They could have played defense for the Soviet Red Army hockey team. They were wearing tight T-shirts, athletic shorts, and track shoes. In Russian accents, they asked to go to Wicker Park. They were in town for the parade.

There were a couple of interesting things to ponder regarding these two comrades. First, they came from a country where the leader oppresses homosexuality and they were now in a country that openly and proudly celebrates its gay citizens. Second, they had traveled halfway around the world, and they were using the same rideshare application that my local patrons use. I found both of those facts to be incredibly fascinating on a crazy day. Another thing about this ride... they were speaking Russian, a guttural language, with a feminine lilt. Pat had to restrain Patrick from cracking up at the unfamiliar flow and cadence being bantered about. They were courteous passengers and Pat hoped they enjoyed our brand of freedom and the pride we have for all Americans.

On the way home a strange thing occurred. Pat entered Patrick's world. It had always been the other way around—Patrick entering Pat's world—and it usually happened at very inopportune times. Pat wondered why there is no Heterosexual Pride Parade, and Patrick quickly told him in an authoritative voice, "That would be boring, you old shit."

HAPPY BIRTHDAY, AMERICA

The Fourth of July fell on a Friday that year, and I had planned to be a dedicated driver for three months, so holiday or not, it was back to the car. I had to come to grips with my feelings about not participating in the festivities, as I had when I first started sacrificing my Friday and Saturday nights for this research. Hell, I'm old, but not dead, and I enjoy a good time, too. I would start early in the day, I decided, and drive until after midnight. It was hot and sunny, perfect for parades, barbecues, and fireworks. The city was basking in the summer sun, and the day would culminate with the city's firework display at Millennium Park. The early part of my shift was a constant onslaught of coolers, strollers, Tupperware, and cases of beer being loaded into and out of the car. I popped the trunk and nicely instructed, "Please put everything in the trunk." There were families, couples, and solo riders. Hi Ho and I provided transportation for the national holiday ritual.

The day was moving at a very fast pace. The iPhone was buzzing and it was always in the high-demand bonus mode. Traffic was terrible, and patience became key. At roughly two in the afternoon, I was called to an apartment building on the Gold Coast. A young couple entered the car with wet hair, as if they had just showered, and gave me an address of a local brunch spot. At this point, I was unaware that I knew this young lady and that I had watched her grow up. She pulled out her phone and made a call, apparently to her brother back home in South Bend. (I lived in South Bend for eleven years.) My ears perked up. She asked him what he was doing for the holiday and she mentioned South Bend family names, all of which I recognized. Then she wanted her brother to say hi to Jack, a guy she had met the night before. She asked Jack his last name, and he told it to her brother. Jack blurted out her first name, which I will not use in the book because it's not a common name.

South Bend is a small town, and as soon as I heard her name, I knew who she was. She had gone through grade school with my sons, I had been in the audience at her third-grade play, and now I was driving her to brunch after she had hooked up with Jack the night before. As her discussion with her brother rambled on, I realized two things: (1) I am older than dirt and (2) you never know who may be driving your rideshare car. I drove away listening to Neil Young's "Old Man." The realization that Pat's sons' third-grade class was not frozen in time pricked his psyche and then nestled itself in.

Pat was driving down Clark Street, and one of his favorite irritants got to him again. The city had recently installed two-foot-high, neon yellow signs with a little stop sign man painted on the side. The goal here was to prevent people from going to the corner to cross a major thoroughfare, as has been the practice since the invention of the automobile. Pedestrians could now cross at will in the middle of a city block. Your car might be traveling at thirty miles an hour, but if someone darts into the street near one of these signs, your job is to slam on the brakes and permit them safe passage.

Well, there I was at one of those signs, and Skippy jogged into traffic. He was tall, about six feet four inches, and his shoulders were at least ten inches wider than his waist. He had donned the latest in gray fitness wear with neon yellow stripes. His hair glistened with gel and perspiration. He forced traffic from both directions to lock up quickly. Casually, he looked to the left and gave a condescending wave, and then repeated the action to the right. As he passed, my imagination took off and I was sure that Skip was engaged to Babs, and that Babs's daddy had a manufacturing company with a fine bottom line.

As I waited in the middle of the block and fantasized about the complete life and persona of a total stranger, I took note, *Now I see why several of those little stop sign men are flattened and part of the pavement.*

The day continued to be a nonstop handoff of containers of egg salad and unopened cases of beer. To prevent people from scratching the paint on the top of my rear bumper, I got out of the car to help transfer their holiday paraphernalia in and out of the trunk. Not that I was doing this for the money, but not once did anybody reach into their wallet or purse to show gratitude for the help. I tend to over-tip because of the endless service jobs I worked in high school and college. Gratuity behavior is something I always observe about business associates and people in general. None were forthcoming this Fourth for an old man lifting cases of beer and picnic supplies.

A buzz came from Rogers Park off of Sheridan Road. There I picked up three women, one in her twenties and two in their mid to late fifties. The youngest of the three sat in the front passenger seat. She gave me the address of a Cuban restaurant on North Avenue, a good distance away. They were quite dressed up for the Fourth of July, and the young lady told me they were going to a farewell party for her aunt, who was moving to North Carolina. We talked about the book I was researching. She confided in me that she had always wanted to write a book. We discussed the process, and how one goes about beginning a career as a writer. We had a great conversation while the two ladies in the backseat talked to each other for the entire ride about various family members who were going to be at the gathering. They were oblivious to the refreshing exchange taking place in the front seats.

We were about two blocks from the restaurant when one of the older women informed the passenger in the front seat that she needed to buy wine because the restaurant was BYOB. As everyone exited the car, I offered to drop the young lady off at the liquor store, no charge, and save her part of the walk on a hot day. I was heading in that direction anyway. One of her matronly relatives turned and gave me a nasty look and said, "Absolutely not!" Ouch—I was just trying to be nice to someone with whom I had just had a pleasant conversation and had just spent $20 on a ride. Pat was only trying to do a good deed. I have to admit, he was quite taken aback by the middle-aged woman's rejection of his attempted act of kindness.

I was back on the road, and packages of bratwurst and foldable lawn chairs continued to invade my world. The work was harder than on any other day of this experiment. A buzz came from Buck Town, where I picked up a young, tanned couple. They were on their way to Millennium Park to meet her friends, and they wanted to stake out early seats for the fireworks. They sat close to each other in the center of the backseat, and we were not yet two minutes into the journey when I heard a sound like two plungers being separated. Oh shit. Here we go again. Hormonal responses for all to hear.

The annoying plunger sound kept popping inches from my ear, and then the mumbling started: "Oh baby, what a great day we've had so far."

She replied, "I'm sorry, sweetie, I had no food for you."

"That's okay, baby. You gave me what I craved and what I needed." Plunger pop. This kept up, and she promised that her girlfriends would have food for him at the park. Ugh. They irked Pat and Patrick alike.

As we drove, Romeo quickly pointed out his place of employment. Betty Crocker cooed, "Who do you work for? What do you do?" Damn. Another plunger pop in my ear. He explained his employment situation while they were face mashing. It was apparent that they didn't know much about each other.

He was excited about taking her to a restaurant in Wicker Park that has fried chicken and porn on Monday nights. (No, that's not a typographical error, and I did not mean "corn.") This puts a whole new spin on the concept of breast, thigh, or drum stick? She was interested in the proposed poultry and carnal adventure.

We drove by the East Bank Club and in an attempt to impress her, he informed her that after his next promotion, he was going to join that club. She replied that every guy she had dated who had been a member of that club had been a superficial jerk. His body language changed with her response, and he replied, "Well, maybe you're right." A chasm was developing in plunger pop land. As we grew closer to Millennium Park, they got closer to their respective car doors. Note to young studs reading the book: Learn a little about your desired before you try to impress her. I drove away listening to Smokey Robinson's "Tears of a Clown."

Pat was in deep traffic near Millennium Park and Patrick became aggressive behind the wheel to get away from the firework-crazed crowd. Pat got to his go-to street, Wells, and it did not fail him. He was soon off to Wicker Park, fleeing the madness of Michigan Avenue. Hi Ho was bouncing all over the north and west side of the city, and everybody was in a hurry to get where they needed to be. I was driving west on North Avenue, about to cross Wells Street, when a guy on a yellow crotch rocket came directly toward me, weaving on both sides of the road, dodging oncoming traffic. Behind him were the flashing blue lights of three Chicago Police Department squad cars. Pulling over, I watched the spectacle pass me, guessing that the guy on the bike had one of two final destinations: Chicago Police lockup at 26th and California, or the morgue.

Still a little shaken by seeing a motorcycle coming directly at me, when I got buzzed to a strange address off of Western Avenue, I hit it. To my surprise, it was a hospital's emergency room. I waited for my fare to appear. After ten minutes, a woman in her early thirties entered the car. She was obviously not feeling well, and she asked if I could drive her to a pharmacy a few blocks away and wait while she had a prescription filled. She made a call, and I heard her say, "But, Momma, between the ER bill and the cab fare, I don't know if my debit card has enough for the prescription I need filled." I slid my hand over and ended the fare even though we had more ground to cover. Hell, I wasn't doing this for the money, and she looked like life was beating her down a bit. We arrived at the pharmacy, and she asked again if I would wait. I looked at her and said, "Yes. No need to rush." I pulled over in front of the drugstore, content to wait for this poor soul, knowing the meter was off.

As I waited, a young man with long, blond dreadlocks, knickers, and a leather satchel sporting an *Occupy* sticker over his shoulder exited the pharmacy. He got on his fixed-gear bike and looked at the car, then me, and proceeded out of the clear blue to give me the finger. Patrick prepared himself to return the kind gesture but Pat stopped him and Pat reminded him: "Now remember, you have to get this sick lady home." As he rode by, Patrick's eyes caught his, and he smiled and nodded. I bet dollars to doughnuts that this clown was a trust fund baby.

The woman came out of the pharmacy and slowly returned to the car. Her address was not that far away. We arrived at her apartment building, and she asked if she could wait and see the final fare. I obliged, so we waited for the phone to compute the charge. The small screen flashed $3.95. I looked at her and said, "I hope you feel better." She had a look of shock and disbelief on her face, and she thanked me as she slowly walked to her door. I drove away listening to Cat Stevens's "But I Might Die Tonight."

Back to the Fourth of July trek. Another buzz right away. Damn it. I have to go back to Millennium Park. This is going to be a cluster fuck. The fireworks had just ended and I was surrounded by pedestrians and crawling cars at Randolph and Michigan Avenues. The crowd of satisfied fireworks aficionados was growing. The customers would not cross the street, forcing me to waste fifteen minutes snaking my way through one-way streets to end up on the side of the street where they were waiting. I picked up the couple with a young boy, and I heard what I did not want hear: "Fifty-first and Michigan Avenue, please." It was hot and humid out, and things were exploding all over the city. I did not want to drive to that neighborhood at this time on this day— or any time of day, for that matter—but they were already in the car.

The little boy was five or six, and he was singing at an elevated volume to his personal audio device, which played loud hip-hop music. My eyes were locked forward as I watched the tenths of a mile tick off the estimated distance function of my GPS. Those were the longest five miles of the night.

The little boy told his mother that he liked Justin Bieber. The mother said, "That's nice, son."

The male rider said, "What are you teaching this boy, woman?

116

Bieber is a racist motherfucking Canuck."

Wow. Tell her how you really feel, I thought.

Three and two-tenths of a mile to go. I swear I hit every red light, and Junior was still belting it out at the top of his lungs. I wondered if waterboarding could be any worse than this situation. The couple was getting increasingly irritated with each other. "I *am* hearing you, stupid bitch," he would say, and she would reply, "You're a stupid motherfucker."

Nice, I thought. *Eight-tenths of a mile to go.*

Finally, we arrived at their destination. The woman and boy left quickly, and the man called after them, "You go on now, and I'll take care of this." He pulled out a twenty and said, "I want to tip you. Do you have change?" Patrick looked at him cockily, and he informed him that the tip was included. They stared at each other for at least thirty seconds. Then the passenger slowly got out of the car. Simply put, never pull out your wallet if you're driving rideshare. It's a good way to get robbed. The next day I heard that several cab drivers had been robbed throughout the city while shuttling holiday traffic.

There I was at 51st and Michigan. It was eleven-thirty p.m. and I wanted to get back downtown. The iPhone was off, and I decided that the best option was to go through Hyde Park and take Lake Shore Drive north back to the Loop. I hit the Drive, and all was well until I passed Soldier Field and traffic came to a halt. Turning the iPhone back on, I saw it was extreme surge pricing time. Leaving the Drive, I got a buzz from Hubbard Street.

Waiting for me was a couple in their late twenties or early thirties. They gave me an address in Evanston. The address was about ten miles away, but traffic was a mess everywhere. The guy was quite talkative, but the woman was almost passed out and whimpering in pain. I asked him if she was alright. The man replied that she had been over-served at the buffet and at the bar. *Great*, I thought. It was going to take us a good forty-five minutes to get to their destination, and she was percolating.

He was obviously well-educated, and he inquired about the car and about me. I told him about the book. He noticed my ring, and I shared with him that I have an MBA. He was eager to tell me that he was a JD, and he named his Ivy League school, and then he told me that sick little Kiley was an MBA/JD from an equally prestigious institution of higher learning.

He wanted to hear the juicy stories of what had happened in my travels. I told him a few stories, and he liked it, almost appearing to get off on my recollections. Meanwhile, poor Kiley was drifting in and out of consciousness, moaning in gastric distress. He commented that if she wasn't so sick, they would love to do something wild and kinky to qualify for my book. Then, in a geeky way, he said, "Could you imagine, a JD and MBA/JD from prestigious schools, doing something crazy to get into your book?" He laughed, which produced a snort and some kind of projectile bodily fluid. I smiled and nodded.

Kiley rose as we completed the S turn entering Rogers Park. I heard, "Morris, I don't feel well," in a faint, agonized voice. Quickly, I pulled over because (1) the sensation of a moving car could not be helping her situation, and (2) I needed to get the plastic bags out of the seat pocket. These were plastic grocery bags and no way designed for the eruption that was about to happen.

We were sitting on the side of the road, and Morris had a bag poised and at the ready. Ms. Kiley started loading bags with enough digested barbeque for a small army. Morris was also aware that there would be a $75 cleanup charge if she redecorated the interior of my car. Quickly, the car reeked of her efforts. So that this would not become a duet, I opened all the windows for relief. Kiley filled bag one, then bag two, and finally bag three. I was so relieved that I had shunned the environment and chosen "plastic" not "paper" at the grocery store. As she was emptying the contents of her stomach, Morris reminded her about the volume of ribs, blueberry pie, and beer that she consumed during that day. He also reminded her how much they had spent on all that food and beer. I looked at the guy. "Do you really think we need a play-by-play?"

Finally, Kiley was done filling grocery bags with vomit. Morris was holding all three. He had a look of amazement, and was totally fascinated by the bags. He turned to her. "Kiley, my sweet, you have ten pounds of bile here."

Looking at the strained, thinning plastic, knowing those bags were not designed for sweet Kiley's precious bile, Patrick directed, "Hey, Morris, there's a trash can over there. Will you please quickly go throw the bags out?"

"Oh yes. You're correct," he said in a dorky manner, and then he clumsily made his way to the trash can.

We continued north to Evanston, and he amused his bride by teasing her that she couldn't hold her beer and ribs like she used to when she was in school. Like she used to? I would hate to have seen this girl at the top of her game back in her heyday. This chick could have stocked every food pantry in the city with what she had packed away.

The entire ride took close to two hours, and finally, we arrived at their hotel. Morris looked at me sadly and said, "I wish we could have done something exciting to get into your book."

Patrick looked at him as he visualized a nasty picture of Morris and Kiley. "Maybe next time. Take care, and think about throwing a little Gatorade into Kiley." The fare totaled $65, which shocked me because I was unaware we were still in a high demand period. Driving away I listened to Joe Walsh's "Life's Been Good to Me."

It was well after one-thirty in the morning, and I was deciding whether or not to trudge on or go home. The situation at 51st and Michigan, the yellow crotch rocket, the fountain called Kiley, Mr. Occupy, and the popping plungers had made a long day substantially longer. I decided to call it a night. I turned the phone off and turned the news on. Driving with the news on the radio with passengers in the backseat can lead to uncomfortable discussions, which was why I always tried to play music in the car, but after a long day of driving, I wanted to know what was happening in the city and around the world. On the local front, the number of shootings in the city was well into the double digits. I didn't know it then, but the final number of shootings in Chicago that holiday weekend would crest at sixty-one, with eleven deaths. This figure would stick in my mind, and it would ultimately lead to the conclusion of this wild ride.

The news was depressing, so I put on some patriotic music. The song was "A Soldier's Joy," performed by Edgar Mayer from his *Heartland* album. This is a traditional American folk song dating back to the Civil War, with roots tracing back to Scottish and Irish fiddling traditions. It's a song that gets your feet tapping and your face smiling. As the music played I thought of all the men and women who have sacrificed so much over the past 200-plus years. I wasn't sure if it was Pat or Patrick that was driving this thought train, but they were both grateful for the opportunity to have the freedom to drive on the Fourth of July. I drove unhurriedly and noticed an illuminated American flag waving in the early morning. I looked up and realized that all the craziness that I had witnessed in the past twelve hours was a beautiful byproduct of our free and open way of life, which we often take for granted. As I pulled into the driveway, Edgar Mayer was performing a string instrumental version of "Amazing Grace." I looked up into the starlit summer sky and said, "Happy Birthday, America."

HOT FUN IN THE SUMMERTIME

It was a week after the Fourth of July, and the realization that the summer season was passing the halfway mark dawned on me. Even at my age, seeing the back-to-school sales in July is still a depressing hint of what is just around the corner.

But hell, that was months away, and it was still summer. Chicago sits on Lake Michigan and boasts one of the most breathtaking waterfronts of any major city. The boating season is short but thousands of spectacular vessels dot the blue water, adding to the aesthetic perfection of the lakefront in the summer. In the world I grew up in, boats were luxuries that you observed from the shore. They were cool to look at, but I viewed them as a prop on the summer stage. My boating experience consisted of a few trips on sightseeing boats for forty minutes at a crack. Still, as a Chicagoan, I loved the fact that the boats were out there, bobbing in the Great Lakes breeze.

Driving had become very routine, and I was beginning to contemplate my Uber retirement date. Another Friday night was upon me, and I was on the prowl. The night started out like any other, going from Lincoln Park to the West Loop. I left the West Loop and drove to Humboldt Park, and so on and so on—nothing interesting or noteworthy, but then, my threshold of what was interesting and noteworthy had been significantly raised over the past few weeks. The streets all looked the same, and I had memorized the stores, bars, and eating establishments on certain roads. The novelty was well worn off, and this had become like any other task-oriented job, monotonous and boring.

The first three hours of the night were dull, but then a buzz came from a neighborhood restaurant and bar, where two men and a woman in their late forties got in the car. They were dressed in business attire, looking as if they had left the office and gone directly out on the town. They had been drinking, and one of the fellas had a shopping bag filled with what appeared to be gifts. I learned that they were attorneys and they were celebrating the recent decision of one of the gentlemen to join a different law firm. The other man and the woman were attorneys as well, but also husband and wife. It all seemed plain vanilla.

We were headed to the address they had given me when the husband of the woman asked if I knew the location of a certain gentleman's club. Before I could answer, his wife had Googled it. They rerouted me in the direction of the jiggle joint. All three were excited about the two men watching the woman get lap dances, which she apparently had enjoyed in front of them in the past. Things went downhill from there. They reminisced about the carnal three-way escapades they had shared in the past. Pat was somewhat disgusted and turned off by the cuckold fetish trio in the back seat. Patrick, naturally, wanted to hear more. They also vowed that their crazy friendship did not have to stop just because Albert was with a new law firm.

We pulled up to the club, and they shot out of the car like three

122

middle school students going to Wrigley Field on a field trip. I drove away listening to the Police sing "Every Little Thing She Does Is Magic."

Little did I know then that this was going to be a night to remember. I was moving at a good clip, driving a lot of nice people who were relishing the evening. Everybody was in a good mood and the night was actually enjoyable. From time to time I played one of my favorite games with the riders. It worked best with young women who were already drunk. By now I knew that most of these kids get liquored up before they go to the bars to keep the cost of inebriation low and manageable. I digress. Back to my game for personal amusement. Usually, riders got into the car and commented about how nice it was and all the other moss. A few times, I'd say, "This is a quiz cab." Immediately, they would look to the roof of the car for brightly colored flashing lights. I would laugh and explain that there were no lights but plenty of quality questions. The best question was "Who is Joe Biden?" The answers I would get were hysterical. Was he the Chicago Cubs' last manager? Was he the first man to land on the moon? Was he a chef on a cooking show? I also learned that Abraham Lincoln was the father of our country, Dr. Joyce Brothers discovered penicillin, and Bill O'Reilly was the quarterback for the New England Patriots. I have to admit, I relished this diversion on dull nights. Good-natured fun, no harm intended.

At eleven-thirty, a call came from an area known as the Viagra Triangle. The Triangle is an upscale hotspot where the older kids play. It's located in the Gold Coast where Rush and State Streets merge, about three blocks south of Division Street. The restaurants are expensive, and they cater to the over-forty-to-over-sixty late-night party crowd. To put it bluntly, there are a lot of five-dollar bills trying to look like fifties in the Triangle, as well as a lot of older people wearing their clothes a bit too tight. The area attracts conventioneers, high-class escorts, and middle-aged folks searching for that second chance on romance, even if only for a night. Most of the restaurants on the Triangle have outdoor dining in the summer months, and even at eleven-thirty p.m., there was not a table to be had. Inside the bars, small crowds were gathered around pianos, where piano players belted out songs and took random requests to fill their fishbowls with cash. Beyond the outdoor tables, parked on the street, there's just about every kind of exotic and expensive automobile. The valet jockeys don't stop. They're a show unto themselves. You can also watch the hotshots slip the valets a twenty or more to have their pride and joy parked in front of a joint to impress the crowds. Big hair abounds, as do the Rolexes, fake and real.

Waiting for me in the heart of all this glitz and spandex were a guy and girl in their early twenties, and a woman in her late forties or early fifties. The guy sat in the front seat and the older woman in the rear passenger seat, with the younger woman seated behind me. They were friendly, and none were feeling any pain. Patrick looked in the mirror and noticed that the older woman was pretty hot for her age: blond, nice figure, with a hell of a tanned and freckled rack protruding out of her low-cut, center-wrapped summer print dress. The younger riders referred to her as "Auntie."

The guy asked if I could stop at a drugstore. He needed cigarettes. So, it was a likely story that the older woman in the backseat was his aunt, as he was very specific about wanting a drugstore, not a gas station, for his cigarettes. *Hell, at least he was practicing safe sex*, I snickered to myself. The two young riders were a bit geeky, but what did I care. He returned to the car from the twenty-four-hour pharmacy, and I was told to go to the pier near Northerly Island, which is an outdoor concert venue on the city's lakefront.

Off we went. They were an extremely talkative lot, yapping about

Auntie's husband, who was in Miami, Florida, buying a bigger boat, and how much fun that would be once the vessel was purchased. We arrived at the harbor, where Auntie's smaller boat was docked. The kids were in a hurry to get to the vessel. Auntie told the kids that she had left her phone at the piano bar, and she needed to go back to the bar and get it. She leaned on the passenger door, straining her dress, and said, "I'm leaving my shoes, so don't take off. Leave the meter running." She left her orange Jimmy Choo platform shoes on the front passenger seat, and she ran up the dock in her bare feet. Patrick noticed that without the platforms she was still attractive, but just not as hot as with the six-inch heels. To be blunt, she now seemed a little chubby. But what did he care? The meter was running.

Patrick waited about ten minutes, and Auntie returned to the car. Her precious shoes that cost about as much as the GDP of a third world country were just where she left them. She sat in the front seat this time and placed her purse on her left side. Patrick glanced into her bag, and what did he see? A glittering turquoise iPhone nestled in her purse. *Okay*, Patrick thought to himself, sporting a perverse grin. *This is going to be interesting*. He asked where she needed to go to retrieve her phone. She told him the address, and they were off. As the car rolled, she became a Chatty Cathy doll. Patrick was sure that in his ten-minute wait, Auntie Golden Globes had had a bump of blow to perk her up. She was leaning over the console and talking a blue streak. She gabbed about her son, who was in London, and her husband, who was off buying another, much larger, boat. She was a free woman for one more week until they both returned home. Patrick listened, and she told him about her career, dropping names left and right. He was smiling and nodding as she speed-talked. Her knees were scrunched on the seat, and he saw that the only thing holding this wrap dress together was a loosely tied cloth belt.

We arrived at the piano bar, and she announced that she'd like another drink and to listen to more music. Then she said, "You're not going to let a lady drink alone, are you? Leave the meter on." Pat thought, *What the hell! Here I am, going into a high-end piano bar where I might see a business associate, and I'm wearing a white T-shirt, blue jeans, and sandals, with her on my arm.* He left the meter on.

As we walked to the piano bar, some guy approached Auntie and gave her a kiss and they talked for two minutes. Pat stood back and waited. She explained, "This is a guy I recently dumped." Okay, Pat was starting to figure this out. This whole situation was about as subtle as a sledgehammer to the face.

We sat at the piano and ordered a few drinks. The guy was playing run-of-the-mill piano bar music. She was happy, until the piano player closed the top of the piano and said, "It's one a.m. I'm done for the night." Then she was sad and began to pout. Pat was relieved and saw himself getting out of this situation very soon.

Not so fast!

We got in the car, and she talked for a minute or twenty. She stuck out her chest and said—I swear this happened—and it is verbatim, "Don't get any ideas about playing motorboat with these girls tonight."

I looked at her and said, "It never crossed my mind." Honestly, it hadn't. If I were a male pig, that was an invitation like no other. I started the car. The meter had been running, and I was ready to return her to the love boat. But no, she perked up, newly re-animated. She had other plans. She knew of another piano bar that was open much later. I knew where it was, and off we went as the clock kissed two a.m.

This piano bar was fairly busy, but we landed seats at the piano. The piano player knew her quite well—surprise, surprise. We ordered drinks and she was happy again, and the meter continued to run back in old Hi Ho, who was getting light duty compared to his trusting,

126

yawning driver. The pianist was really good. There wasn't much he didn't know, and he felt comfortable playing contemporary songs, as opposed to "Oklahoma" and "When I Was Seventeen." I was enjoying this guy's selection of music and feeling a mild buzz. Auntie kept filling his fishbowl, and danced alone in the corner with her Jimmy Choos under her stool. Hell, she was having fun, and I was getting an interesting story. Plus I was listening to good music. *What could be so bad?* I thought. I do have to admit that I was worried about hubby coming home early from his boat-buying excursion, but the more she talked, the more I realized they didn't spend too much time together. Time flew by as the piano player played memorable tunes from the seventies, eighties, and present, and...so we closed another piano bar. The lights came on, and it was time to get the princess back to the harbor before her pumpkins turned into coaches.

Back in the car, the meter had timed out because I hadn't been there to hit the refresh button. No great loss. I think it died at $50. I started driving back to the harbor. She was sitting on her knees in the passenger seat, and the belt on her dress was starting to loosen. We entered the dark parking lot at the harbor a little after four a.m. She was clutching my arm, with her head on my shoulder. *Shit*, Pat said to himself, *How am I going to untangle this mess?* We pulled up to the ramp by the pier, and she leaned back. The dress was fully open, and I saw that, like many of her younger contemporaries, she was sans lower undergarments and sporting hardwood floors. The difference between her and her younger counterparts was that she was like a well-broken-in Wilson A2000 baseball glove—the kind of baseball glove every young boy dreams of.

She leaned over and tried to kiss me. Pat stopped her. "You're smoking hot and I've had a marvelous time, but my heart belongs to another, and it would not be the right thing to do."

Patrick tried to argue his case for a change in attitude, and he pleaded with Pat, *Are you sure about this, dude?*

She sat up, grabbed one of my cigarettes, and lit it. She cracked the window, and with her dress totally open and wearing nothing but a bra underneath, she looked at me and said, "You're going to pass on this?"

I smiled and nodded. "Yes, I am, and the sun is coming up soon, so I'd best head home."

She gave me a big kiss and asked, "Why couldn't I have met a loyal guy like you?"

It might be because I don't own a boat, I figured.

Driving away, I listened to Steely Dan's "Dirty Work." I thought about the old saying that every action has an equal and opposite reaction. Not once all night did her phone ring from hubby. From eleven-thirty to four-thirty a.m., not one "Good night" or "How are you doing?" call from anyone. Pat also wondered how many times in his past relationships he had behaved the same way to someone. Patrick was infusing Pat with doubt and insecurity. The mythical creature Patrick was mythical no more, but was now in total control of Pat's emotional state. The birds were chirping as I pulled into the driveway. I wondered how someone so beautiful, who apparently possessed so much, actually had so little.

At two-thirty in the afternoon I woke up. I was quiet and depressed all day because of the activities of the night before with my blond, music-loving friend. I decided to hell with getting the car cleaned, and tried to unloosen the knots in my shoulders, neck, and legs by taking a sauna and a whirlpool at my club. After the club, I decided to have a late lunch with my two sons. Normally in the summer our discussions are spirited, and the topics revolve around who they're training with for the upcoming college hockey season, what courses they're planning on taking, and potential graduate school opportunities.

The boys talked, and I sat there not participating, just staring out the sandwich shop window. Then I noticed three young girls in tight yoga pants entering the back seat of a sedan. Patrick then interrupted Pat. *I wonder where those skanks are off to?*

Pat quickly reprimanded Patrick in their private world. *"Skank?" Really, "skank?" Patrick, I haven't heard that word since high school, you jerk.* Pat tried to rejoin the conversation with his sons, but at that point he realized there was a stormy tug-of-war being played out inside of him. Time with his sons had always been precious to him. He knew they would be leaving soon for Boston and Minneapolis. But Patrick would not let go of his grip on Pat. He was like a third child, wanting attention. Pat didn't realize that this psychological war would cost him dear relationships in the other areas of his life after this experiment stopped. The lunch was a failed exercise. Patrick had conquered Pat.

I realized that the past three months were catching up to me. Now when I wasn't driving, every time I saw a young woman on the street or in a store, I envisioned her throwing up in my car. After last night, I could also add another depressing image to the mix. Every time I saw an attractive, middle-aged woman, she was opening her dress and giving me a flash in the front seat of my car. I closed my eyes and saw angry boyfriends, pissed-off bicyclists, and irate cab drivers cutting off their mothers to get a lane. I heard the lies about addresses and late-night banquets. This exercise that some people might consider fun, exciting, and erotic was starting to destroy my view of humanity. My personal compass was askew. I was emotionally flat and intellectually lifeless from this three-month fandango. My actions felt mechanical, my emotions numb. Not a good place.

Six p.m. came and went, and I decided not to venture out until about seven-thirty. I was in no hurry. There I was, all hooked up, ready to go, as I slowly backed out of the driveway. Gone was the explorer spirit I'd had in May. I headed down Belmont Avenue, and the obnoxious buzzing began. One rider after another was delivered to where he or she wanted to go. I was not very talkative, and neither were many of the fares. Maybe they were projecting my negative aura back to me. As the night progressed, I functioned in a totally removed state. I didn't mentioned the upcoming book to anyone. I just drove.

The streets were crowded, and every aspect of the night was a struggle. Contrary to my usual practice, I kept the news on and listened to the reports of the local shootings and fires of the past twenty-four hours. I listened to sports. Both the Cubs and Sox were in the shit, making the contents of the evening sports report pure noise. I zoned out, but was brought back to focus by the cracking sound of my right front wheel rim hitting a deep pothole that I had tried to avoid for the past three months.

Sitting at a red light, I noticed two other rideshare drivers. One was a young man having a good time, and the other was a man older than myself who appeared to be petrified. What are the people who do this for a living or to augment their incomes actually pulling in financially? I did the mental math again to remind myself. After completing a cost accounting analysis, I had discovered that after covering gas, insurance, wear and tear, and maintenance, these poor drivers were barely making fifteen dollars an hour. I thought about the risk of hauling strangers. I shook my head and I wasn't smiling. I knew that soon I would open the newspaper and read of an amateur rideshare driver found slumped over the wheel, lifeless, in some remote parking lot.

Not one smile or positive thought did I express during the first three hours of driving that night. A police car would drive by, and I would think of the amount of unfunded pension liabilities plaguing the city police pension fund. This thought would lead my negative stream of consciousness to the cheerful fact that Chicago was fiscally not far behind Detroit, Michigan, which had recently filed for bankruptcy protection. The next cheerful mental jump pertained to the unionization of rideshare drivers. I was on a mental death spiral.

Pulling over, I got a cup of coffee and gave myself a good talking-to. It was after eleven and I had been a miserable jerk to myself and everyone who had entered my car. After that, I picked up a few fares and I forced myself to be pleasant. Bit by bit, I started to feel something like my old self and the people appeared to be getting friendlier as well.

Next buzz—North Michigan Avenue, where an elderly, well-dressed couple was at the curb waiting for me. They directed me to "41st Street in Maywood, please." This address was due west, with no chance of a return fare on the way back.

"Great," I grumbled. We made our way to the Eisenhower Expressway. I knew this trip would be a good hour-and-a-half round trip. Then I tuned into their conversation. The two were criticizing everything about the meal they had just eaten.

"Oh, his execution on the pasta course was terrible, and the sauce with veal had no flavor," the overweight lady declared.

The guy, sporting a bow tie, was "simply, simply, simply disappointed with everything." Then in unison, they destroyed the wine selection and complained about how it was totally out of sync with the courses. The next areas they attacked were the décor of the restaurant and the quality of the floral arrangements. The woman then shared with her bow tie-clad escort that she had told the owner that everything was *divine*, and they simultaneously cackled with forced laughter.

I almost ran off the road when they blurted out, "It was a good thing that we didn't have to pay for the meal."

They had been at the soft opening of a new restaurant. A soft opening is akin to a dress rehearsal for a play, where the mistakes are supposed to be made. Constructive criticism is expected and fundamental to the exercise, as well as to the future of the establishment hosting the dinner. Pat was incensed to think that someone had valued their opinion, and they had not been honest when it came to this critical business exercise. They continued to chat, not saying one positive word during the entire wretched ride.

We were off the Eisenhower Expressway, and began the slow trek through small suburban towns, keenly aware of the local speed limits. I was counting the streets: 31st Street, 35th Street, and finally, 41st. I turned down the side street, which was lined with small, older, well-kept homes. The lady piped up and directed me to the Tudor on the right with the lights in the front yard. I pulled up to a small home with a Tudor façade and a lawn adorned with at least ten illuminated lawn gnomes. *Tasteful*, I evaluated.

They left the car without saying another word, not even thank you. She waddled up the sidewalk with her doggie bag in hand, and he skipped alongside her. I guessed that they didn't sleep in the same bedroom.

Slowly, I drove back to the expressway, increasingly mindful of the speed traps. I headed back to the city, deciding what time to wrap up for the evening. It was well after one a.m., and the upbeat trip to Maywood had almost driven me back to my early evening funk. I decided to see how I felt when I exited at North Avenue from the Kennedy Expressway.

The ride was fast, and I would soon be back in my comfort zone of the Near North Side of the city. I was not off the exit ramp yet when the iPhone buzzed, just as it had hundreds of times over the past three months, summoning me to a bar in—where else?—Wicker Park.

I pulled up to the bar, and, as usual, a couple in their late twenties or early thirties was staring at their smart phones, waiting for their magic carpet ride to appear. They got in, and I asked, "Where to?" The burly white guy, reeking of booze, gave me an address in west Lakeview. Tired, I just wanted to focus on the road.

The woman was sobbing, "Can you at least be discreet when you're trying to pick up another woman?" He didn't say a word as he brooded, looking out the rear window, losing himself in the passing traffic. She asked, "When does it end, Bill?" He turned his shoulder so his back was facing her as he continued to stare out the window. The lady continued to weep, and the guy continued to ignore her. I drove in silence, with nothing on the radio. I could hear the treads on my tires attack the cracked asphalt. The problem was that they weren't attacking fast enough.

He turned and said, "Enough with the fucking crying." He raised his voice and said it again.

She responded by declaring, "I'm finished with you."

The next thing I knew, from a sitting position, this guy delivered a roundhouse right hook to her jaw. I almost hit an oncoming car. I reached into the pouch on the driver's door as I pulled the car over. The Taser was then engaged for the last time. Patrick so wanted to plant his 4,000-volt friend on this moron's genitals and press so hard that the bastard would never reproduce. The burly slob was perplexed, his bravado fading quickly as he cringed when I turned around, pointed the Taser at him, and said, "Just get out." I repeated in a loud, angry voice, "Get out. Now." The accumulated angst and rage of the three previous months was almost at an uncontrollable level. I just wanted to explode on this asshole.

He looked at her and said, "Come on, bitch."

Pat said, "No, she can stay if she wants."

Patrick wished the Taser had the Glock 43 option.

He got out, and I left him there at Western and Fullerton Avenues. I drove the weeping woman to the fourth district police headquarters, walked her in, and explained to the officer on duty what had happened. She wanted to file a police report. The police took it from there, and I left in disgust over what had just transpired in the back of my car.

Getting back into my car, I turned off the phone for the last time. In one weekend, I had seen pathetic loneliness, ungrateful envy, petty jealousy, and savage force. I drove home in stunned silence. I recalled that my father had never raised his hand to my mother. It was engrained in the men in our family at a young age that you never raise your hand to a woman. I kept hearing the man's fist connect with the woman's jaw, causing a helpless scream. It was repulsive and something I knew I would never forget. All in all, for this old man, as Sly would say, "It was hot fun in the summertime."

REQUIEM FOR THIS RIDESHARE DRIVER

I pulled into my driveway, closed my eyes, and sat alone in silent darkness for at least five minutes. The faces of the past three months were projected in my mind. I heard the sounds of the loud drunks and the people singing with the music. I smelled the sweat, vomit, and perfume that polluted the air of my car. I saw a man lying on the pavement with blood flowing out of his punctured skull. I saw tired people after work, happy people with newfound love, and sad people with broken hearts. I heard hope from young men and women and lies from the deceitful in the same crowd. I turned over in my mind the belief that a person's word is his or her bond, and I considered that in my lifetime I had witnessed two presidents lie on television: "I am not a crook" and "I did not have sexual relations with that woman." We are an extremely developed and wealthy society, but we have lost our innocence and, sadly, our word. I saw the human condition intimately manifested in a four-door sedan. This three-month experiment had changed me more than any relationship, any course, any degree, or any other significant event in my life.

I lifted my sore tailbone and inflamed right leg out of the car as an Uber driver for the last time. Normally, I would take out the iPhone, GPS, Taser, and bulletproof back pad, put them in the blue bag given to me months before, and leave them in the trunk of trusty Hi Ho. That night, however, I packed everything in the blue nylon bag, brought it into the garage, and placed Patrick, the rideshare driver, on a shelf, as if he were entombed in a mausoleum.

The house was quiet as Pat made his way to the ever-waiting balcony to try and absorb all that had happened over the last few hours. No scotch tonight. Pat just leaned on the railing overlooking the river and stared quietly. "Enough," he said.

Patrick said, "But dude, this is a ride on the wild side."

Then Pat yelled at Patrick out loud, "Enough!" At that point, Pat realized he was alone, and he was yelling at the weak and sick side of his own personality that had grown over the past three months. Patrick had shaken Pat's foundation, which was now brittle. This might have been repairable if Pat were younger. The hardened callous of over fifty years of living, which can dull, but protect our senses, had been ripped off, exposing a wound raw and painful, only without the benefit of a full lifetime in front of him to heal. Pat could not decipher who was the antagonist and who was the protagonist within.

Pat stood motionless as the river reflected the moon like a piece of glass. "Fuck the self-impressed people I do business with. Fuck those assholes who rode in my car. Fuck relationships. Fuck trust. Fuck the concept of love, and most of all, fuck me for doing this to myself," Pat confessed out loud to no one. I feel displaced from my normal work environment, I'm too old to comprehend the shit that I've witnessed, and the prime of my life has past. I'm screwed. Pat's right leg twitched with pain. His stomach felt as if he had eaten steal shavings, and the last fragments of his emotional strength had been shredded.

He closed his eyes and again saw a kaleidoscope of images from his novel, cool urban experiment: a man bleeding on a street, a pair of horn-rimmed glasses forecasting his future, a woman being punched, an insecure girl looking for acceptance, sucking off a self-absorbed guy in a vestibule, and a wife satisfying her husband's voyeuristic tendencies. He re-heard the countless lies and falsehoods. In his quest for data, he had found out how little his psyche could tolerate, as well as how sad a buzz ride society can deliver. He leaned against the railing and realized that he himself had done many of the things that had him so rattled, and that what he was experiencing was the realization of his own flawed human condition.

Watching all this unfold from the removed position of a driver's seat painfully churned the caldron of shit in his own heart and soul. Patrick is as much Pat as Pat is Patrick. Seeing this behavior and not participating was akin to observing the first derivative of human behavior from his older eyes and aged constitution with painful memories of his behavior as a younger man, which only brought him back to the underlying variable of the derivative, himself. Pat's mind's eye then hosted a requiem for his generation. The youth movement of the sixties had inherited a prosperous, opportunity-filled nation from their parents' "Greatest Generation," only to then fuck it up with their McMansions and excessive debt.

It took three months to blow my mind in so many different directions. The world has changed so much and so damn quickly. The advances in technology are moving so swiftly that we're living in dog years. If we go back to the invention of electricity and the many new inventions that soon followed, such as electric lights, radio, and ultimately television, the changes seem insignificant compared to what has happened over the past thirty-five years. Yes, radio and television were improved over sixty years, but they were still relatively the same technology, except for bluer blues, redder reds, and more channels than we could possibly stomach. Since the creation of the affordable personal computer in the early eighties, all bets have been off. The PC was put on steroids as the internet became the backbone of our society. This new form of instant connectivity made revolutionary changes in our lives. The ways we communicate, recreate, procreate, travel, bank, and so on have all been reduced to bits of data.

From driving these young people from one place to the next, I realize they have it all in the palm of their hands—literally. I won't dwell on this, but let's take music as just one example. In college, my generation lugged hundreds of vinyl albums around in orange crates along with speakers the size of end tables and three to four cumbersome components, all of which would fill a mid-sized sedan. Not anymore. People now have thousands of songs downloaded on their phones and a pair of ear buds in their pockets. They have their agendas, contacts, money, directions, games, and naked pictures on that three-by-four-inch blade. This has created a totally portable, disposable, and data-driven generation. To dump a "friend," just send him or her a text and delete them from your contacts, substantially less risky than having to look someone in the eye and explain why she/he is no longer significant in your life.

The world to Pat's matured eyes is now like a snow globe, and when you shake it bits of data and bandwidth come falling in a blizzard of "my generation will define your generation's future." The bottom line is—as Pat has to admit, to Patrick's dismay—that Poindexter is right, even though he was quite rude. People over forty are hostage to technology, and the children of the Nixon, Johnson, and Vietnam periods are not cool anymore. We are our parents. The thought that one's own generation is no longer relevant is difficult to comprehend as the baton is past to the next group of energetic women and men.

The "love children" of the sixties and seventies are like a bookmark left in the early chapter of a book that was completed a long time ago, and which now sits in the clearance section of a used bookstore. This is what I learned behind the steering wheel of my car.

To quote Chicago, from one of their earliest songs, "Lowdown": "Oh, my life has passed me by, the country I was brought up in fell apart and died. Oh no, love no longer there, cold wind blew away the sun that used to warm the air, low down, feeling pretty bad, feeling like I lost the best friend I ever had." Come on. You had to expect at least one song from Chicago in this book.

Pat thought of all the older rideshare drivers whose careers were castrated due to the advent of new technologies. *No gold watches for them,* he thought. He was spent and scared as the river continued to reflect the moon and his memory reflected nothing but sobering and sordid thoughts. The sun slowly broke through the early morning sky. Even though there would be no more fares, Pat realized that this ride was a long way from being over.

For the next few weeks, I needed to decompress. Briefly, I thought about chucking it all, buying a slushy machine, and living on a beach in L.A. I would just listen to music on my headphones, smoke weed, and sell slushies. It sounded like utopia. Then reality hit me. The boys were still in college, and with my cardiovascular system trashed, this was probably not a good solution. Reading became one way to control the stimulation to which I had been subjected, and I found solace in an excerpt of a poem by Walt Whitman, "Transpositions," from *Leaves of Grass.*

> *Let the reformers descend from the stands where they are*
> *forever bawling – let an idiot or insane person appear on*
> *each of the stands;*

Let judges and criminals be transposed – let the prison-
    keepers be put in prison – let those that were prisoners
    take the keys;
Let them that distrust birth and death lead the rest.

These words of role reversal, helped center my off-balance view on life created by Pat and Patrick. After my meltdown, I drove my car only when it was absolutely necessary. I stayed to myself, and I tried to reconcile how detached from everything and everyone I felt. My traditional weekday pursuits were a chore, and I put off as much work as I could. I even shunned the stock market for a month. It took several weeks before I digested all that I was exposed to during my short Uber career. I tried gradually to regain my normal way of life and accept the world around me. The changes I experienced had taken root in my core, and I knew they had established permanent, but hopefully, a manageable residence.

REFERENCES

Music

10CC. "The Wall Street Shuffle." *Sheet Music*. UK Records, 1974. CD.

10,000 Maniacs. "My Sister Rose." *In My Tribe*. Elektra, 1990. CD.

The Beatles. "Helter Skelter." *The White Album*. Apple, 1968. LP.

Browne, Jackson. "Boulevard." *Hold Out*. Asylum Records, 1980. CD.

Browne, Jackson. "Doctor My Eyes." *Jackson Browne*. Asylum Records, 1972. CD.

Brubeck, Dave. "Take Five." *Time Out*. Columbia Records, 1959. LP.

Bowie, David. "Suffragette City." *The Rise and Fall of Ziggy Stardust and the Spiders from Mars*. RCA Records, 1972. CD.

Burdon, Eric and War. "Spill the Wine." *Eric Burdon Declares War*. MGM, 1970. CD.

Cale, J.J. "Cocaine." *Cocaine*. Shelter, 1976. CD.

Chapin, Harry. "Taxi." *Heads and Tails*. Holtzman, 1972. LP.

Chicago. "Lowdown." *The Very Best of Chicago: Only The Beginning*. Warner Strategic Marketing, 2004. CD.

Cline, Patsy. "Crazy." *Showcase with the Jordanaires*. Decca, 1962. LP.

Crosby, Stills, Nash & Young. "Almost Cut My Hair." *Déjà Vu*. Atlantic, 1970. CD.

Crosby, Stills, Nash & Young. "Teach Your Children Well." *Déjà Vu*. Atlantic, 1970. CD.

Dire Straits. "Skateaway." *Making Movies*. Vertigo, 1981. CD.

The Eagles. "In the City." *The Long Run*. Asylum, 1979. CD.

The Eagles. "Life in the Fast Lane." *Hotel California*. Asylum, 1977. CD.

The Eagles. "Take It Easy." *Eagles*. Asylum, 1972. CD.

The Eagles. "Take It to the Limit." *One of These Nights*. Asylum. 1975. CD.

Electric Light Orchestra. "Hold on Tight." *Time*. Jet, 1981. CD.

Grateful Dead. "Franklin's Tower." *Blues for Allah*. Grateful Dead, 1975. CD.

Hawkins, Edwin. "Oh Happy Day." *Let Us Go into the House of the Lord*. Pavilion, 1967. LP.

Hot Chocolate. "You Sexy Thing." *Hot Chocolate*. RAK, 1975. CD.

Joel, Billy. "Travelin' Prayer." *Piano Man*. Columbia, 1974. CD.

Joplin, Janis. "Mercedes Benz." *Pearl*. Columbia, 1971. CD.

Lewis, Jerry Lee. "Great Balls of Fire." *Great Balls of Fire*. Sun, 1957. LP.

Lewis, Jerry Lee. "Whole Lot of Shakin' Going On." *Great Balls of Fire*. Sun, 1957. LP.

Meyer, Edgar. "Soldier's Joy." *Heartland: An Appalachian Anthology*. Sony BNG Music, 2001. CD.

Meyer, Edgar. "Amazing Grace." *Heartland: An Appalachian Anthology*. Sony BNG Music, 2001. CD.

Miller, Roger. "King of the Road." *The Return of Roger Miller*. Smash, 1965. LP.

Mott the Hoople. "All the Young Dudes." *All the Young Dudes*. Columbia, 1972. CD.

Petty, Tom. "I Won't Back Down." *Full Moon Fever*. MCA, 1989. CD.

Pink Floyd. "Comfortably Numb." *The Wall*. Columbia, 1979. CD.

Police, The. "Every Little Thing She Does Is Magic." *The Police*. A&M, 1979. CD.

Police, The. "Walking on the Moon." *Reggatta de Blanc*. A&M, 1981. CD.

Question Mark and the Mysterians. "96 Tears." *96 Tears*. Cameo-Parkway, 1966. LP.

Rabbitt, Eddie. "I Love a Rainy Night." *Horizon*. Elektra, 1980. CD.

Reed, Lou. "New Sensation." *New Sensations*. RCA, 1984. CD.

Reed, Lou. "Walk on the Wild Side." *Perfect Day*. RCA, 1972. CD.

Robinson, Smokey. "Tears of a Clown." *Make It Happen*. Hitsville USA, 1970. LP.

Rolling Stones, The. "Brown Sugar." *Sticky Fingers*. Rolling Stone Records, 1971. CD.

Rolling Stones, The. "Sad Sad Sad." *Steel Wheels*. Rolling Stone/Columbia, 1989. CD.

Sayer, Leo. "Long Tall Glasses." *Just a Boy*. Chrysalis/Warner Bros., 1969. LP.

Sly and the Family Stone. "Hot Fun in the Summertime." *Fun*. Epic, 1969. LP.

Steely Dan. "Dirty Work." *Can't Buy a Thrill*. ABC, 1972. CD.

Stevens, Cat. "But I Might Die Tonight." *Tea for the Tillerman*. Island, 1970. CD.

Walsh, Joe. "Life's Been Good." *But Seriously, Folks*. Asylum, 1978. CD.

Young, Neil. "Old Man." *Harvest*. Reprise, 1972. CD.

Movies

Driving Miss Daisy. Dir. Bruce Beresford. Prod. Richard Zanuck and Lili Fini Zanuck. Warner Bros., 1989.

The Godfather. Dir. Francis Ford Coppola. Prod. Albert S. Ruddy. Paramount Pictures, 1972.

Goodfellas. Dir. Martin Scorsese. Prod. Irwin Winkler. Warner Bros., 1990.

Mr. Peabody & Sherman. Dir. Robb Minkoff. Prod. Denise Nolan Cascino and Alex Schwartz. Twentieth Century Fox, 2014.

Television Shows

Breaking Bad. Exec. Prod. Vince Gilligan, Marie Johnson, and Michelle MacLaren. High Bridge Entertainment, 2013.

Mad Men. Exec. Prod. Matthew Weiner, Scott Hornbacher, Andre Jacquemetton, Maria Jacquemetton, and Janet Leahy. AMC Studios, 2007.

Saturday Night Live. Exec. Prod. Lorne Michaels. NBC, 1975.

Books

Davis, H. *Works of Plato (Part I, The Republic)*. New York, NY: Tudor, 1933.

Frost, Robert. *Robert Frost's Poems*. New York, NY: St. Martin's, 1971.

Whitman, Walt. *The Complete Poems of Walt Whitman*. Ware, Hertfordshire: Wordsworth, 2006.

ABOUT THE AUTHOR

Intense, can't-shake-it curiosity led **Pat White** (a pseudonym) to drive for Uber after researching his growing interest in ride-sharing and other disruptive and "new economy" businesses for a possible *Harvard Business Review* article. Pat's articles on technology and strategic communication have been published in professional business journals.

Pat began working in 1979 for the Chicago Board Options Exchange before becoming a retail stockbroker for some of Wall Street's largest firms. In 1996, he received an MBA in management. He went on to work for the business college he graduated from, focusing first on executive education and then serving as director of the university's for-profit media company, where he showed his skill at rescuing ailing organizations.

The lifelong Chicagoan was president of a technology company owned by a founder of a prestigious leverage buyout/private equity firm on Wall Street before returning to Chicago after an eleven-year hiatus in Indiana. He has managed money for Hollywood celebrities and advised some of Chicago's most influential families and businesses in the areas of turn-around management and strategic bus iness growth.